craft

your own

happy

**A collection of 25 creative projects
to craft your way to mindfulness**

craft
your own
happy

A collection of 25 creative projects
to craft your way to mindfulness

BECCI MAI FORD

*Photographs by Jesse Wild
and Becci Mai Ford*

WHITE OWL

*Thank you to my husband Mike for your patience
with my mess making, craft supply addiction and
for helping me to photograph things late at night.
Your support and love made this book possible.*

First published in Great Britain in 2020 by
PEN & SWORD WHITE OWL
An imprint of Pen & Sword Books Ltd
Yorkshire – Philadelphia

Copyright © Becci Mae Ford, 2020
www.hellohooray.com @hellohoorayblog

ISBN 9781526747396

The right of Becci Mai Ford to be identified as Author of this work has been asserted by
her in accordance with the Copyright, Designs and Patents Act 1988.

A CIP catalogue record for this book is available from the British Library.

Group Publisher: Jonathan Wright
Series Editor and Publishing Consultant: Katherine Raderecht
Art Director: Jane Toft
Editor: Katherine Raderecht
Photography: Jesse Wild and Becci Mai Ford
Styling: Jaine Bevan

Printed and bound in India, by Replika Press Pvt. Ltd.

Pen & Sword Books Ltd incorporates the Imprints of Pen & Sword Books
Archaeology, Atlas, Aviation, Battleground, Discovery, Family History, History, Maritime,
Military, Naval, Politics, Railways, Select, Transport, True Crime, Fiction, Frontline Books,
Leo Cooper, Praetorian Press, Seaforth Publishing, Wharncliffe and White Owl.

For a complete list of Pen & Sword titles please contact:

PEN & SWORD BOOKS LIMITED
47 Church Street, Barnsley, South Yorkshire S70 2AS, England
E-mail: enquiries@pen-and-sword.co.uk
Website: www.pen-and-sword.co.uk
or
PEN AND SWORD BOOKS
1950 Lawrence Rd, Havertown, PA 19083, USA
E-mail: Uspen-and-sword@casematepublishers.com
Website: www.penandswordbooks.com

contents

introduction

I live my life by making lists. I save lists on my phone, scribble lists on scraps of paper and even email lists to myself. My obsession with lists started at a very young age. I've always been a bit of a worrier and making notes was my way of trying to manage all the thoughts in my head. The trouble with making so many different lists is that it all gets a bit disorganised and I start to worry that I've written something important down somewhere and then forgotten about it!

It was only recently that I realised my racing thoughts and the reason that I feel the need to incessantly write things down is due to anxiety. I'd had a week of sleepless nights worrying about my business and despite writing all my anxieties down, my mind still couldn't rest. By the end of that week I was a tired crying mess. I was burnt out and something needed to change.

I'd heard the term 'mindfulness' batted around the internet for several years, but I'd never thought of it as anything other than a new craze or trend. It turns out, folks, that mindfulness is actually a very important tool to protect your mental health. It's about making the time (even if it's just for a few minutes) to give your mind a rest and shift your focus on to what is important in life.

Making things has always been a passion of mine. I began to realise that I was at my calmest when I was crafting. The internal noise of all my thoughts and worries would quieten as I forced my mind to focus on the activity at hand. I used crafting as a mindfulness activity. This discovery led me to start my small business, Ellbie Co, and I started to create kits of my favourite craft activities for people to make at home.

I like to think of this book is an extension of my craft kits. Unlike other craft books, this is a book that you can dip into and find projects based on how you are feeling. So, you can craft to suit your mood! There are lots of beginner-friendly projects to choose from including cross stitching, embroidery, paper craft and more. The best way to use this book is to choose the chapter that best describes how you are feeling and then pick a project. The majority of projects in this book can be picked up and put down, so even if you only have a few minutes to spare you can still enjoy a moment of mindfulness.

I set up Ellbie Co. in 2017 because I couldn't find the sort of happy cute craft kits that I wanted to make. Since I launched my business, I've sold my kits at crafting events across the country and online. Everything is created in my tiny rainbow-filled space in Sussex. So far, I've been making this journey up as I go along and I've loved every minute of it!

I hope this book helps you to find your own form of mindfulness and bring you some happiness on a cloudy day. If you are feeling worried and anxious, you are not alone. Reach out, talk to somebody and try to be kind to yourself.

See this book as permission to spend time dedicated solely to you.

Craft your own happy!

Love Becci xox

the basics

GETTING STARTED

At first glance, embroidery can look very complicated. Don't worry, it's not! You can create some beautiful effects and very detailed work with just a needle and some embroidery thread. There are hundreds of different embroidery stitches you can learn, from the simplest of stitches to complicated stitches that take time to master.

As a beginner, don't be put off from starting any of the embroidery projects in this book. Yoou really only need to learn three basic stitches to get you started. Every embroidery project in this book only uses these three stitches. Step-by-step stitch instructions are in this chapter and you can refer back to them if you find that you get a bit stuck on any of the projects.

Embroidery is very addictive so once you've started you will probably want to learn more!

HOW TO SET UP AN EMBROIDERY HOOP

Embroidery hoops aren't essential, but I think they are a very useful tool for beginners. If you are new to embroidery, you may find creating a steady tension on your thread tricky. Your thread tension will vary and this means the fabric you are embroidering can twist out of shape.

Using an embroidery hoop keeps the tension of your fabric even right from the start. I think that embroidery hoops also make lovely frames to display your work when you are finished too.

You can pick up an embroidery hoop from most craft stores and haberdashery shops; they are quite cheap and come in a wide range of sizes and materials. I personally prefer to use bamboo wood hoops because they are lightweight and if I feel like decorating the hoop, they tend to be very quick and easy to paint.

1. The first step in setting up your embroidery hoop is to unscrew the hoop and remove the outer ring.

2. Lay the inner ring of the hoop on a hard surface. Lay your fabric on top of the inner ring, push the larger hoop over the inner ring and fabric, and gradually tighten the screws at the top of the hoop.

3. Tap your fingers on the front of the fabric and when it sounds like a drum, the tension is right and you are done. Don't trim the excess cotton fabric yet; you might need those extra bits later.

STITCHING TIPS

Once your hoop is set up you are ready to start stitching. You will need embroidery thread which can be found easily in any craft store. Embroidery thread comes in skeins, which tends to be approximately 8 metres in length. A skein is more than enough to finish any of the embroidery projects in this book.

Embroidery thread comes in a huge range of colours and you'll also find metallic and sparkly glitter embroidery threads. Whatever colour you choose, it will always consist of six strands of embroidery thread.

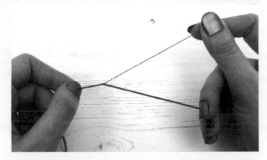

1. The first step is to separate your embroidery thread; you will only be using two strands to stitch with. **2.** Firstly you need to cut a length of your chosen thread and hold this length with one hand.

3. Pinch the end of one of the strands with your other hand and slowly and gently pull the strand up and out until it is separated from the remaining strands. Pull one stand at a time as pulling multiple strands can cause your thread to knot.

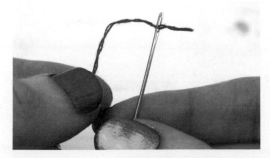

4. Once you have two strands separated, pinch them together and thread your needle.

5. If you are a beginner, I advise you tie a small knot at the end of your thread. Try not to make a large chunky knot as this may cause a bulge underneath your fabric. You are now ready to start stitching!

SATIN STITCH is a simple stitch designed to fill in large blocks of colour. You can use it to colour in areas of your design or to create text with a bold appearance.

1. Start by bringing the needle up through the fabric at your chosen start point in the design.
2. Insert the needle into the fabric across from your original entry

point on the opposite side of the area you are filling in.
3. Bring the needle back up where you started through the fabric on the opposite side.

4. Repeat this process, coming up and going back down on the opposite side of your fabric, as you fill in the area of your design.

BACK STITCH creates a solid line and is useful for embroidering small details such as text or outlines. You can also use backstitch to create your own shapes and free stitch onto your fabric.

1. Begin by pulling the needle and thread up through the fabric and make one small stitch forward.
2. From underneath your fabric, mark out the length of your

desired stitch with your needle and then pull it back up through the fabric. Bring the needle and thread back down through the end of the previous stitch.

3. Continue to make small stitches, making sure there are no gaps between each stitch to keep your work looking neat and tidy.

RUNNING STITCH will be used in projects where some sewing is required rather than as an embroidery stitch. This stitch is one of the most basic stitches you use.

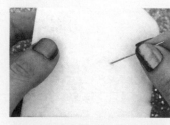 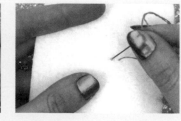 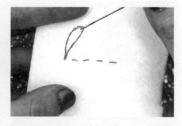

1. Begin by pulling your threaded needle up through the fabric.
2. Insert the needle back down through the fabric close to where

you pulled it up. Pull the thread back down to complete your stitch. **3.** Now insert your needle back up through the fabric,

leaving a space from the previous stitch. Pull the needle back down through the fabric again to make your second stitch.

FRENCH KNOTS are slightly more difficult than other stitches, but they are worth the extra effort! They add interesting texture to your work and can be used to fill in small or large areas of your design or to create details such as flower centres.

1. Bring the needle up through the fabric and, with your non-needle hand, pinch and hold the thread taut near where it exits the fabric.

2. Wind the thread around the needle once or twice (the more times you wind it around the needle, the bigger the knot).

3. Pull the coil of thread taut and then reinsert the tip of the needle back into the fabric close to the exit point.

4. Continuing to pinch the thread, give it a small downward pull so that the coil tightens and slides down the needle.

5. With the coil in position on the fabric, push your needle all the way through to secure it in position. You have just completed your first French knot!

If you have ended up in a tangle of thread, don't worry! French knots can be a bit tricky to master; just go back to step one and start again until you get it right.

FINISHING YOUR WORK Once you have come to the end of your stitching, you will need to finish it off before you cut your threads or your design might unravel or look messy.

1. Secure your thread by first tucking your needle back through the last few stitches that you made.

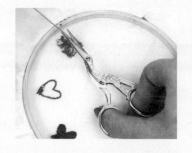

2. Using embroidery scissors, trim excess thread being careful not to cut too close to your design.

chapter one: anxiety makes

We all need to take a step back and take a bit of time out every now and again. The world can be a pressurised and fast paced place, which isn't always the best thing for our mental health. Take a little time out with these longer projects; they are designed to be made gradually, a bit at a time, at your own pace on those days when you feel a little anxious and you need a moment of peace. Crafting is the perfect distraction for a busy mind.

You can't do it all

We live in a world full of pressure. Whether it is the pressure to look a certain way, or to live a certain lifestyle, the pressure to be 'living your best life' is everywhere. It is impossible to do it all so instead we end up with a constant nagging feeling that we are failing in some way or another. It's really no surprise that the majority of people will experience some kind of anxiety at one point in their lifetime.

I always saw myself as being very mentally strong. I knew who I was and I was confident in my own skin. I never really thought of myself as being somebody who had anxiety until about 2013. I had just left university and things started to go a little bit wrong. The pressure to work out where I fitted into the world, family troubles and a bereavement meant that I was worrying, but on another level to how I had felt before; my thoughts would race at night, I'd struggle to breathe and at times it felt like the weight of the world was closing in on me. Anxiety is hard to explain to anyone who hasn't felt it – it's more than just feeling a bit stressed or worried; an anxiety attack can leave you feeling like you are dying.

I would get stuck in a spiral of not wanting to leave the house, which led to me not exercising, which then led to not sleeping and that led to my anxiety worsening. Round and round this cycle would go until I would have an anxiety attack.

I learned that the key to preventing this downward spiral into anxiety was to distract my mind. This sounds easier than it is. It's not as simple as just sitting and watching the TV; instead you need to really engage in an activity so intensely that you can only focus on that one thing, rather than your racing thoughts.

This state of concentration is otherwise known as 'flow state'. You can achieve flow state through all sorts of activities. Personally, I find talking things through, running, hula hooping and crafting are my favourite ways of finding flow. But it's all about trying a mixture of different activities to see what works best for you. You don't always need to spend ages doing a flow activity. A little bit of time every day is enough, so even if you only have ten minutes to spare it's worth it.

The crafting projects in this chapter are designed to be worked on bit by bit. They use repetitive crafting techniques that make it easier to settle into flow state. These projects allow you to spend a few minutes a day relaxing, making and hopefully giving your mind something else to focus on, rather than your anxiety.

daily ritual embroidery

Finding time for yourself every day can be tricky; there are so many life admin tasks, job stresses and social activities to juggle. But even a few minutes dedicated to a mindful activity like embroidery can help to relax the mind.

Time required:
Take as long as you want to on this project and just enjoy the journey!

You will need:
- Embroidery hoop (3" or 8cm)
- Embroidery thread
- Sewing needle
- Plain cotton fabric (7"x7" or 18x18cm)
- Felt square (7"x7" or 18x18cm)
- Embroidery scissors
- Template (see templates chapter)
- Transfer paper (optional)
- Pom pom trim (optional)
- Iron
- Imagination

Sometimes the journey is more important than the end result! The great thing about embroidery is that it is very easy to pick it up and put it down without losing your place. This project isn't meant to be completed in a few hours or even in a few evenings; this is a daily embroidery project for you to spend just a few minutes a day stitching. You can either use the abstract template in this book or make up your own design and pick any colours that you like.

INSTRUCTIONS

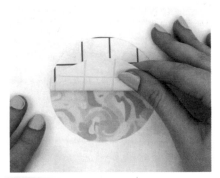

1. Start by photocopying the abstract template design on to the transfer paper. Cut around the design as neatly as you can (try not to leave a large border around the edge).

2. Put your fabric on the ironing board and, following the manufacturer's instructions, use a hot iron to gently press the transfer on the fabric. Peel the backing paper off to leave the design.

3. You are now ready to place your fabric into your embroidery hoop. If you don't have a hoop to hand you can still make this project, but it might be a little bit trickier to stitch. To learn how to set up an embroidery hoop, go to the basics chapter at the beginning of this book.

5. Separate the strands of your embroidery thread and thread your needle. Tie a small knot at the end of the thread.

6. Now your hoop is set up and your needle threaded, you are ready to start embroidering.

7. You can choose a variety of different stitches to complete your design. For larger areas satin stitch is a great way to flood spaces with deep vibrant colour.

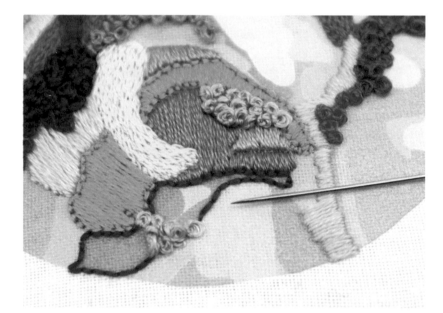

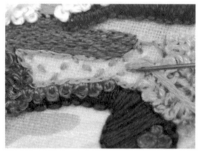

9. Another great use of back stitch is free stitching. Because it is such a fine and detailed stitch you can use it to create your own shapes and patterns within your design.

8. For finer details, backstitch is ideal. You can also use backstitch for the edges of the coloured satin stitch areas to make them really stand out. You may find that you need to move the fabric around the hoop to reach areas on the edge of your design. Don't be afraid to undo your hoop and move the fabric around to reach those tricky edges; you can always move the fabric back into position at the end.

To create an interesting texture, you could choose to make rows of backstitch side by side in a small area. However, be warned, this will take a long time so whilst it can look stunning, only do this for a large area if you are willing to spend a lot of extra time stitching!

10. French knots are slightly trickier to master but are worth it because they will create a beautiful 3D texture on your design.

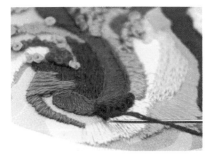

11. You could try filling larger areas of your piece with a variety of different sized French knots to create a varied texture.

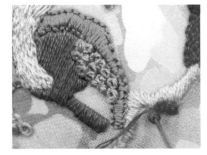

12. To enhance your piece even further you can also scatter French knots in the spaces between other stitches to add extra detail.

13. Once you have finished, finish off your stitching by passing the needle under three completed stitches to secure the thread.

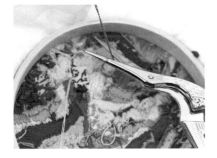

14. You can now trim any remaining threads, but be careful not to cut them too close.

15. The final step is to back your hoop. Firstly you need to trace around your hoop on to the felt and cut out the circle.

16. Thread a needle with enough thread to go all the way round the fabric in your hoop. Tie a large knot in one end and sew around the fabric with big running stitches.

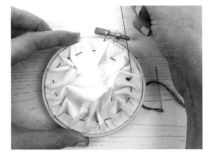

17. When you have finished, pull the thread to gather the fabric in towards the centre. Secure with a large knot close to the fabric.

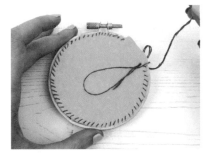

18. Put the felt on the back of the hoop and stitch it to the gathered fabric, using angled stitches to ensure you catch the fabric.

19. You have finished! You could also try adding some pom pom trim around the edge or painting the hoop using acrylic paint.

flower wall decoration

Making this flower wall was something I wanted to do for some time. Choosing the silk flowers was exciting as there are so many different textures, shapes, colours and sizes to choose from. You'll love how easy this project is to make!

Time required:
This project takes 1-5 hours to make (depending upon the size of your frame)

You will need:
- Scissors
- Shadow box photo frame (any size you like)
- High density foam cut to the same size as the inner part of your frame and the thickness of your frame
- A selection of silk flowers or faux plants (anything with a stem works well)
- Hot glue gun
- Utility knife
- Cutting board

I am sure like me you have seen those amazing Instagram flower wall photos and just thought wow! But did you know that they are more than just a pretty decoration? Flowers can help to create a calming atmosphere, which is great for helping to soothe an anxious mind.

This project is easy-peasy and only takes a few hours to finish. Unlike those Instagram flower walls, this project uses faux flowers so you can have a calming piece of floral wall art to keep forever.

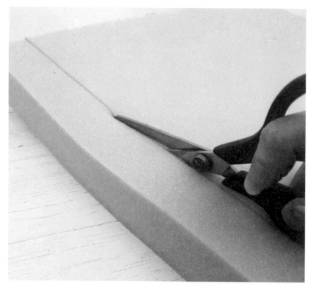

INSTRUCTIONS 1. Place a cutting board on a hard surface and put your piece of foam on top. Take the inner card frame from your shadow box photo frame and lay it on the foam. Use a marker pen to trace round the inner part of the card frame on to the foam.

2. Using a pair of scissors cut along the lines that you have drawn, and cut out your foam piece.

3. Take a hot glue gun and glue the foam inside the photo box frame. Press down on the foam for a few seconds to help the glue to stick properly.

4. Next, select the flowers that you would like to use for your wall decoration. A mixture of colours and sizes of flower tends to work best.

5. Using your scissors, cut down the stems of your chosen flowers. You need to leave approximately 2-3cm of stem per flower to stick them to the foam.

6. Now comes the fun part! Press the flower stems into the foam. For larger flowers, apply a small blob of hot glue to the base of the flower for added security.

7. Continue to press all of your chosen flowers into the foam working from edge to edge until you cover the whole surface. You can now hang your finished piece on a wall to admire!

needle felted unicorn keyring

The first time I tried needle felting I was amazed that you could turn wool into such a wide variety of shapes. There is also something surprisingly therapeutic about gently stabbing a piece of merino wool repeatedly!

Time required:
This project takes roughly 3 hours to make.

You will need:
- ◼ Foam pad
- ◼ Felting needle
- ◼ Merino wool tops (cream, mixed bright colours, light pink and light yellow)
- ◼ Eye pin
- ◼ Jump ring
- ◼ Gold sparkle thread
- ◼ Sewing needle
- ◼ Glue
- ◼ Embroidery scissors
- ◼ Metal keyring chain
- ◼ Tiny plastic eyes
- ◼ Needle-nosed pliers

If you are feeling full of nervous energy and unsure what to do with your time, then needle felting might help. Needle felting involves using a sharp needle to stab gently at wool to make the fibres interlock and form shapes. Repeatedly stabbing at the wool will help release any nervous energy, whilst at the same time the repetitive motion helps you to get into an almost meditative state of concentration. It is a really easy form of crafting and very satisfying to do – just be very careful with your fingers!

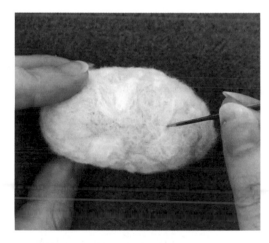

INSTRUCTIONS

1. First lay out your foam pad on a hard flat surface. Take a medium piece of the cream wool and roll it into a ball. Using the needle, gently stab the cream wool, twisting the ball as you do so, to ensure that you are stabbing evenly on all sides of the ball.

2. Keep doing this until you have a firm ball. The wool should now be firm and coarse rather than light and fluffy. If you want the ball to be a bit bigger, you can always add more wool, and continue stabbing and shaping it until you reach the size you desire.

3. Now take two smaller pieces of the cream wool and roll these into two cylinders. Pinch each cylinder in the middle and fold them in half.

4. Using your felting needle, gently shape the two folded cylinders into triangles. These will be your unicorn's ears.

5. Once you have finished shaping your unicorn ears you should have two firm, rounded triangles. To attach the ears to your unicorn, place them on top of your round ball with roughly a thumbs width between them. Using your felting needle, gently stab around the whole base of your first ear pushing it into the round ball until it is firmly attached. Then repeat for the other ear.

6. Take a small piece of each of your coloured merino wools. Roll these pieces of wool together to form a single thick rainbow strand for the unicorn's mane and tail.

7. Roll this rainbow strand out to roughly 10cm in length and cut off one third to use for the unicorn's mane. Put the rest of it aside to use later on in the project.

8. Curve the mane in between the ears and slightly down the back of the ball. Then, using your felting needle, gently stab the wool until the mane is attached.

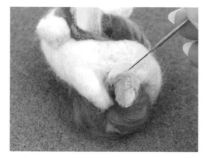

9. Take the remaining piece of the rainbow strand and gently stab this into position near the base of the ball, curving it around the back to form the unicorn's tail.

10. To make unicorn's horn, gently roll a small piece of the light-yellow wool into a cylinder. Stab the cylinder using your felting needle until it is slightly firm.

11. Fold the cylinder in half and twist the two halves together. Lightly stab the horn all the way around to attach the two halves to together. This is your unicorn horn.

12. Thread your needle with the gold sparkly thread and tie a knot in it. Push the needle from the bottom to the top of the horn.

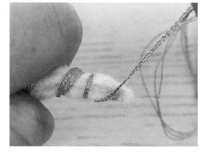

13. Tightly wrap the gold thread around the horn to create definition. Tie a knot in the thread at the bottom of the horn.

14. Attach the horn between the ears by gently stabbing it into place using the felting needle.

15. Using a small bit of light pink wool, carefully roll two pieces into tiny balls and gently attach these to the cheeks of the unicorn, flattening them as you do so.

16. Using the sharp end of your embroidery scissors carefully push them into the ball just above the cheeks to make two small holes for the unicorn's eyes.

17. Place a tiny amount of fabric glue on the end of each of the plastic eyes and press these into the holes that you have just made.

18. Now it's time to attach your keyring. Apply a tiny amount of glue to the base of the eye pin and carefully push the pin into the top of the unicorn.

19. Leave the glue to dry overnight. Using needle-nosed pliers, attach the jump ring to the eye pin and then attach your key ring chain. Your unicorn is done!

relaxing rainbow cross stitch

I first got into cross stitching when I was seven years old, but I didn't finish a project until I was in my early twenties. Now I find it is a really satisfying craft to do, which is why I started designing my own patterns.

Time required:
This project takes roughly 3-4 evenings to make

You will need:
- 14 count Aida cross stitch fabric (7"x7" or 18x18cm)
- Template (see templates chapter)
- Embroidery hoop (5" or 13cm)
- Embroidery thread
- Sewing needle
- Felt square (7"x7" or 18x18cm)
- Pom pom trim (optional)
- Strong glue (optional)

If you are new to needlecrafting then cross stitch is an ideal place to begin. It's surprisingly easy and as you get used to forming stitches, you will find that like knitting and crochet, it can calm the mind. The repetitive motion of cross stitching is very relaxing.

The rainbow in this cross stitch pattern is a reminder that if you are facing tough times they won't last forever. Rainbows are a sign of hope and happiness and hopefully this pattern will bring you both of those things. If you want to mix up the colours and make your own alternative rainbow, go ahead and create your own version.

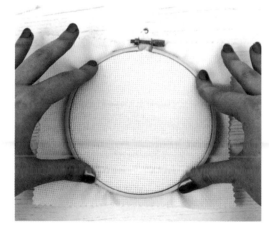

INSTRUCTIONS

1. The first step is to place your Aida into your embroidery hoop. If you don't have a hoop to hand you can still make this project, but it might be a little bit trickier to stitch. To learn how to set up an embroidery hoop, go to the basics chapter at the beginning of this book.

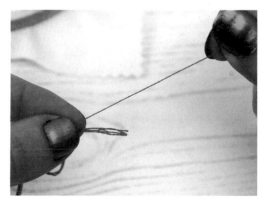

2. Separate out two strands of embroidery thread and thread your needle before you tie a small knot in the end. Once your hoop is set up and your needle is threaded, you are ready to start cross stitching.

3. Starting at the centre of your Aida fabric, bring the needle up through the back of the hoop, leaving about an inch of thread at the back. You will secure this tail of thread with stitches.

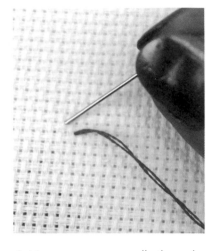

4. Now pass your needle through a hole diagonally across from where you started. This makes a slanted half cross stitch. Hold on to the tail at the back of the fabric so that it doesn't slip through.

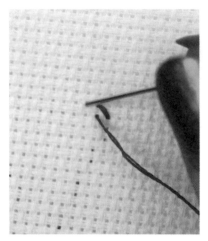

5. Bring the needle up through the hole directly below the one you last used. Before you pull this stitch through, flip your hoop over to make sure the thread tail is trapped by the stitch.

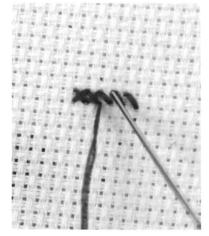

6. Follow your pattern, continuing to stitch along the row to make a line of half stitches. Now go back across the row making a series of half cross stitches in the opposite direction. Congratulations! You have just completed your first row of full cross stitches.

7. Check your pattern to count how many stitches you need to make, remembering each coloured square represents one stitch. Use a marker pen to colour in each square as you stitch so you keep track and don't lose your place.

8. Keep stitching each colour until you have created your rainbow. Keep your stitches neat and your tension even for a uniform look.

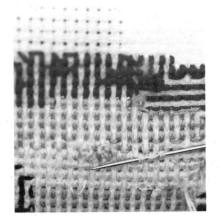

9. Once you have finished stitching, finish off your thread by passing the needle under at least three of the completed stitches on the underside of the fabric.

10. You can now trim off any remaining threads, but be careful not to cut them too close to your fabric or they will unravel.

11. The final step is to back your hoop. To do this, first trace around the hoop on to your chosen felt and cut the circle out.

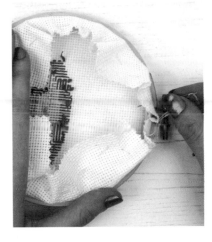

12. Thread a needle with enough thread to reach all the way round your hoop. Tie a large knot in one end and sew all around the edge of the back of the Aida with large running stitches.

13. When you have finished, pull the thread to gather the fabric in towards the centre. Secure with a large knot close to the fabric.

14. Cut out a circle of felt the same size as the hoop. Put the felt on the back of the hoop and stitch it to the gathered Aida fabric, using angled stitches to ensure you catch the fabric. You are done!

chapter two: get outside

Mother Nature is a calming presence in all our lives but sometimes we forget to step away from our screens and enjoy what she has to offer. Simply by going outside and breathing in some fresh air your perspective can shift and your mood will lift. The projects in this chapter all use elements of nature and are designed to encourage you to take a trip outside. This is your excuse to go on a nature walk, explore your local area and enjoy the calming effects of the great outdoors!

enjoy nature

Going outside and enjoying the beauty of the natural world can help to put things into perspective. I live on the south coast of England. One of my favourite things to do when I'm feeling overwhelmed is to take a walk to the beach and look out at the sea. It's such a vast entity that it instantly makes me and my problems or worries feel smaller. Not everybody can head to the beach, but there is always natural beauty around us no matter where we are in the world; it's just up to us to go outside and find it!

It can be hard to motivate yourself to leave the house sometimes, especially if you are feeling stressed out. We make excuses that there isn't enough time in the day, that we need to run this important errand or that we have to do that final thing on our to do list. We don't do these things though. Instead we end up just sitting and stewing in our worry until the end of the day. Being somebody who works from home, I am particularly guilty of this.

If we all just made ourselves take half an hour to go for a walk outside or just to go outside and enjoy our environment, it would allow us to step away from our stress for that time. The exercise and fresh air can actually help us to think more clearly. I find that my half hour moment outside, is a golden time for coming up with new and exciting creative ideas.

The makes in this chapter of the book all contain things that you would find in nature. My aim when designing these projects was to give you the motivation to get outside and collect the materials that you need to create these makes.

I want you to see these projects as a guilt-free reason to abandon your to do list and go outside and enjoy nature!

clay leaf ring dish

When writing this book, I wanted to create a simple project that would bring the outside in and evoke happy memories. This leaf dish is that project. It is a simple make requiring just a few materials but the end result is beautiful and practical.

Time required:
This project takes 15 minutes to make and 24 hours to dry

You will need:
- Air dry clay
- Leaves with big veins
- Curved dish lined with tin foil
- Rolling pin
- White acrylic paint
- Gold acrylic paint
- Dark green acrylic paint
- Paint brush
- Clear glaze
- Sharp knife
- Dental floss (optional)

These little clay leaf bowls are perfect for holding jewellery and other trinkets. They are a lovely way to preserve a part of nature and memories from a recent walk or day out. I think big leaves with thick veins work best for this project but feel free to use any that take your fancy.

I use these little dishes to bring some of the outside inside my home. I have one by my front door for spare change and my keys, one on my bedside table to put my rings when I go to bed and one for my house and car keys.

INSTRUCTIONS

1. Make sure your surfaces are fully protected before starting. Using the dental floss, cut a piece of the air-dry clay. You will need a medium sized chunk, the right size will fit snugly in the palm of your hand.

2. Roll out the clay to roughly 1½ cm in thickness using a rolling pin. Next, carefully take your chosen leaf and press it into the clay with the veins facing downwards to leave a clear imprint.

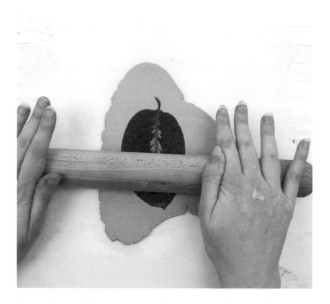

3. Roll the rolling pin over the clay and the leaf to ensure you get a deeper imprint of the veins.

4. Use a sharp knife to gently cut around the leaf imprint on the clay. Cut away excess clay and save it for a future project, and then peel off the leaf.

5. Curve the edges of your clay leaf upwards using your fingers. Make sure you do this gently so you don't distort the shape of your leaf.

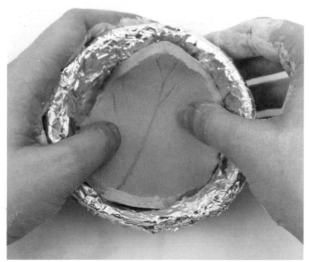

6. Place your clay leaf inside a foil lined bowl and curve the edges upwards. You can do this as much or as little as you like. Leave your clay leaf to dry completely for 24 hours.

7. Yay! Your clay leaf should now be completely dry. Remove it from the bowl. You can leave it naked or paint it – it's up to you.

8. If you are going to paint your leaf, I recommend using a flat brush to ensure you get into all of the veins of your leaf. Using a base of white acrylic paint before applying any other colour ensures your colours will look nice and bright.

9. If you want to embellish your leaf, you can also use a small brush and some metallic paint to edge your leaf dish and to highlight any additional details.

10. Once the paint is dry, you can either leave it matt or use a clay sealant to give your dish a shiny finish. Apply this liberally over your dish with a paintbrush.

gratitude stones

As a child, I collected stones and shells when we went to the beach. I loved how they felt in my hands as I gripped them; their weight and their coolness against my skin was calming. That memory helped me create this project.

Time required:
15-30 minutes plus drying time of 4-5 hours

You will need:
- Stones
- Paint brushes (one medium and one fine small detailed brush)
- Acrylic paint
- Varnish
- Pencil

Becci's tip:
When you pick your stones, bear in mind that you will be painting on them later. Smooth rounded flat stones tend to work best because they have a nice even surface to paint on. However, odd shaped stones can be fun to work with as you can adapt your design to fit the shape of the stone and give it some real character.

Being grateful for the things that you have in your life is a fantastic way to ground yourself, help to focus on the good things and live a happier life in general. Take a stone in your hand, squeeze it and, whilst doing so, think about all the things that you are grateful for. It's an instant pick me up that you can build into your daily mindfulness ritual.

These gratitude stones are lovely little makes to gift yourself when you need a pick me up or to leave in secret hidden places for strangers to find to brighten up their days too!

INSTRUCTIONS

1. The first step is to get outside and get some fresh air! Get off the sofa, step away from your phone and go outside. Take a walk somewhere that you haven't been before. Use this as an excuse to explore, to get lost for a few moments without feeling guilty for taking some time out to do something just because you want to. Listen to the sounds around you and soak up the joy of being alive and living in the moment.

Here I am going for a walk near Brighton beach to collect my stones!

2. Once you've chosen your stones, use a pencil to sketch out your chosen design. Choose a phrase that's important to you, a dot work pattern, a sketch of your favourite animal or even just a cute smiley face!

3. Protect your work surface as acrylic paint can be hard to remove. Using a small paintbrush fill in your design with your chosen paint colours It's easier to fill in the larger areas of colour first.

4. Once the larger areas of colour are touch dry, use a finer tipped paintbrush to add any details using white or black paint. Pick out any highlights or outlines to add interest to your stones.

5. Leave your stones to try completely for 4-5 hours. Then seal in the paint by using a clear varnish. Brush it on the stones in a thick layer and leave to dry for another 3-5 hours.

ocean scene resin necklace

I wanted to create something with real meaning so the tiny shells and sand in this necklace are from Perranporth in Cornwall, where we used to go on our family holidays. It's extra special to be able to carry those memories around my neck.

Time required:
15 minutes plus 24 hours drying time

You will need:
- Jewellery bezel (with a back)
- Sand
- Shells
- Seaweed/plants (optional)
- Glitter/gold leaf (optional)
- Chain with lobster clasp attached
- Epoxy two-part resin (art resin works best for this)
- 5 x lollipop sticks
- 5 x plastic cups
- Tweezers
- Parchment paper

It's so relaxing to watch waves break on the shore. Looking out to sea makes you realise how small you are compared to the ocean and I think that really helps to make your worries shrink away. The beach is a place to think and contemplate; it's a place of calm.

Not all of us are fortunate enough to live by the sea, but you can use your beach treasure finds to make this beautiful necklace and preserve your favourite holiday memories.

INSTRUCTIONS

1. Put down parchment paper to cover your work surface.

2. Check the instructions on the back of your resin box and read all safety warnings thoroughly before use. Then mix a small amount of the resin in one of the plastic cups using a lollipop stick to stir, following the manufacturer's instructions. Depending on your choice of resin, you might need to stir this constantly for 2-5 minutes. Don't worry if your resin contains lots of bubbles during the stirring process; these should disappear as you continue to stir.

47

3. Put your bezel upside down on the parchment paper. Using a lollipop stick, pour a very thin layer of clear resin into the bottom of the bezel and then arrange the sand on top of it.

4. Add the seaweed, shells and any other details to your ocean scene. Leave it to cure for 3-4 hours until the resin is jelly-like. This thin layer of resin will hold your ocean scene in place when we add more resin.

5. Repeat step 2, and using the lollipop stick add more resin to the bezel little by little, making sure the whole beach scene is covered. Be careful not to get resin on your hands or the outside edge of the bezel.

6. If you have any bubbles in the resin, gently blow on them and they will disperse, making sure not to disrupt your scene. If it has moved, use tweezers to adjust your design and then leave it to cure for 24 hours.

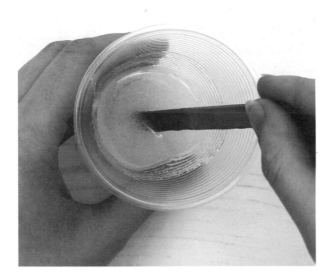

7. Check the resin in your bezel is fully cured. Repeat the process you have used previously for making resin and make another small portion in your remaining plastic cup.

8. Gently pour this resin into the front of your finished bezel. This will dome your design and give it a beautiful shine. Leave to cure for 24 hours. If you want a matt finish, leave this step out.

9. Once your resin has cured, take your chain and thread it through the top of the bezel. Your necklace is finished – wear your piece with pride and soak up the compliments!

pressed flower phone case

I love flowers and I wanted to find a way to preserve their beauty forever. When I discovered resin I was delighted to find that I can have beautiful natural flowers with me all year long and not just when they are blooming.

Time required:
1 hour plus 24 hours drying time. (+3-5 days for pressing/drying the flowers)

You will need:
- Heavy books
- 2 sheets of A4 paper
- Pressed dried flowers
- Flat, solid white iPhone case
- Clear craft glue (PVA glue works well for this)
- Tape
- Scissors
- Parchment paper
- 1 clear plastic cup
- 2 wooden lollipop sticks
- 50/50 clear-casting epoxy resin (art resin works well for this)
- Acetone (or a nail polish remover with acetone)
- Cotton buds
- Glitter/confetti (optional)

A beautiful sunny day (or, if you live in the UK, a beautiful day without rain!), gives you the perfect excuse to go for a walk and collect some flowers. Flowers can symbolise many things, but primarily they are just beautiful to look at and the old-fashioned art of pressing fresh flowers is an easy way to preserve their natural beauty.

This pressed flower phone case shows off the vivid colours of flower petals and adds a pretty touch of nature to your phone! You can use any species of flower, but I personally think ones with smaller heads work best in this project.

INSTRUCTIONS

1. Start by picking your flowers. You can either use ones from your own garden, wild flowers or even use some from a bouquet! Remember though, smaller flowers work best for this project.

2. Place your flowers between two sheets of A4 paper and then place this between two heavy books. You can put extra weight on top of the books to speed up the pressing process.

3. Leave the flowers to press for two days, before removing them. Remove the top sheet of A4 paper and lay the sheet of paper containing the flowers in a sunny place to dry out for about 3 days.

4. When dry, arrange your flowers on the back of your phone case. Bear in mind that your pressed flowers will become slightly translucent once they are coated in resin, so put lighter coloured flowers underneath darker ones for the best effect.

5. Once you are happy with your design, gently glue your flowers on the back of your phone case. Be careful not to use too much glue.

6. Now it's time to add your resin. First protect your surfaces with parchment paper and make sure you are working in a well-ventilated area.

7. Mix your resin in the plastic cup, following manufacturer's instructions. Stir it using a wooden lollipop stick for 2-5 minutes. Don't worry if you see lots of bubbles forming, these will disappear later. If you want to add glitter, do it now.

8. Once your resin is mixed, leave it to rest for 5 minutes. Put your phone case on the parchment paper with the flowers facing up. Pour a small amount of resin onto the back of the case, fully covering the flowers. Pour it in small amounts to make it easy to control the flow of resin.

9. Use a lollipop stick to gently push the resin around the case and fill in any gaps. Make sure all the flowers are covered and lightly blow on any bubbles that show up on the surface to help them disappear. Clean up any spills using a cotton bud dipped in acetone.

10. Leave the case to dry for 24 hours. Once the resin has dried, double check that all of the flowers are fully covered. If there are still gaps, you may need to add more resin. You can do this easily by just repeating the previous steps. Then you're done!

chapter three: happy home

Home. Its your own private dance space, it's your cooking space, it's where you hang out with friends, it's where you celebrate birthdays, play games with your children, cuddle your pets and watch cheesy TV shows on the sofa. But, most importantly, your home should be your sanctuary. The projects in this chapter are all designed to help you add your own personal touch to your home and create a happy place full of self-expression. Even if you are renting, you can still turn your home into a space that reflects who you are.

Sanctuary with personality

Home is meant to be your sanctuary. Your home has a huge influence on your mood and stress levels; it's where you should feel safe. Your home is the space where you can put your feet up and watch TV in your pyjamas. Most importantly, you home is the space where you are free to fully be yourself.

Too often we are sold the idea of a 'perfect home'. You only have to spend a bit of time looking at Pinterest boards to be overwhelmed with images of 'ideal living' expectations filled with expensive furniture and tidy minimalist spaces. But does a perfectly designed space really make a home happy?

For me, I think a happy home is a home that doesn't live in the pages of interior design magazines. A happy home is where you have made your own mark on the environment. A happy home is a place where you can look around and see the love and meaning in the objects surrounding you and a place that actively connects with your personality.

It can be difficult to put your stamp on your home environment, especially if you are renting and confined by a strict set of landlord rules. But it is still possible to make a space feel like your own through making crafted pieces to add warmth and personality. The projects in this chapter of my book are all designed to be I weuked to suit your personal home style so feel free to change the colours and materials as you see fit!

By making these happy home projects, I hope that you will be able to make your mark on the space you live in and turn your home into a happy sanctuary that lifts your mood.

THE OBSERVER'S BOOK OF BUTTERFLIES

BUTTERFLIES

kawaii concrete planter

No happy home is complete without plants! You can't help but smile at this little planter with his smiling face and succulent green hair-do. This is a great beginner-friendly project using cement which is a fun and easy crafting material to use.

Time required:
This project takes 2 hours to make and 24 hours to dry

You will need:
- Silicone concrete mould
- Cement mix
- Gold, black, white and pink acrylic paints
- Paint brush
- Varnish
- Water
- Lollipop sticks for stirring
- Disposable bowl to mix cement in (ice cream tubs work well)
- Vaseline

Caring for plants can be a relaxing experience once you know how to keep them alive! I never had much of a green thumb until I discovered succulents and now I can't get enough of them. They are almost indestructible.

Having plants around your house creates a calming environment to help you cope with any work-related or day-to-day stresses. These little planters are an easy make and a cute way to introduce a bit of greenery to your home.

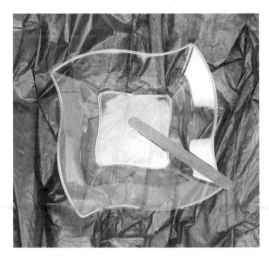

INSTRUCTIONS

1. First cover any surfaces you will be working on to protect them. This project will get messy!

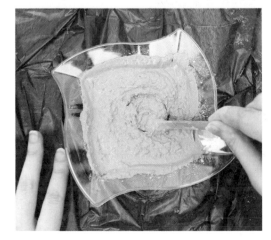

2. Take the cement and mix it according to the packet instructions. Stir it with a lollipop stick, gradually adding water until it forms a thick liquid consistency, similar to cake batter.

3. Rub a thin layer of Vaseline around the inside of your silicon mould. This will help you to get the concrete out of the mould when you have finished.

4. Pour the cement mix into the mould and put in to one side to set. Leave it for 24 hours.

5. Once it has set, remove the planter from the mould. It should just pop out very easily. Make sure it's completely dried. If not, leave it for a few more hours. You can opt to leave it bare if you prefer the rustic concrete look or paint it.

6. I chose to paint mine with a layer of gold acrylic paint, applied with a brush. To add some additional texture you can sponge the paint on instead. Leave it to dry thoroughly before moving on to the next step.

7. To create the face on the side of the planter, first use a pencil to lightly sketch out the facial features. I think the simpler the better with these cute plant holders.

8. Using a fine paintbrush carefully paint the cheeks, eyes and mouth. When the eyes are dry, go back with some white paint to add the highlights. Leave to dry.

9. Once it is thoroughly dried, you can apply varnish in thin coats over the top. This will protect your paint against water damage. Leave to dry.

10. Put some soil in the plant pot, and pop your chosen plant inside. Succulents work well, but you can also use flowers and any other small plants.

pom pom footstool

Pom poms are brilliant little makes that are satisfying to do and are also a great way to use up any leftover yarn scraps that you might have lying around. Once finished, the texture of this footstool is lovely and soft to rest your feet on.

Time required:
This is a long relaxing project, perfect for making in front of the TV. It can take a few days to make.

You will need:
- A range of coloured yarns – I used 12 balls of 100g yarn
- A pouffe or footstool with a removable or knitted cover
- Yarn needle
- Scissors
- Pom pom maker in 3 sizes

Pom poms always remind me of my childhood! Pom poms were one of the first things that I learnt how to make, they are full of vibrancy and joy and they are a brilliant easy make when you don't have much time to spare.

This footstool is a big project, but it's easy to make and can be done little by little over a period of time. It's a great way to up-cycle a piece of furniture into a colourful statement piece, perfect for a lounge or cosy reading corner!

INSTRUCTIONS

1. The first step in making your pom pom footstool is to pick your colour palette. I think a really big range of bright colours works best but that's just my taste. Do feel free to chose a more muted pallet or work with a smaller number of colours. It will look just as beautiful.

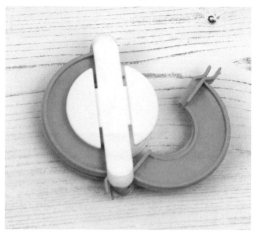

2. Next you will need to make lots and lots of pom poms in a mix of sizes. Set up your pom pom maker by opening up the rings and placing them on top of each other, as shown here. Choose your wool and, following manufacturer's instructions, wind it around to make a pom pom.

3. Each time you finish a pom pom, carefully cut open the pom pom along the outside gap in the pom pom maker using your small embroidery scissors.

4. Secure each pom pom with a length of yarn (20-30cm) tied in a tight knot several times around the centre of the pom pom.

5. Remove from the pom pom maker and neatly trim the edges of your wool, being careful not to cut the yarn around the middle of it. You'll need that later.

6. Repeat steps 2-5 until you have a lot of pom poms in different colours and sizes, all with lengths of yarn around the middle to secure them.

7. Take your first pom pom and thread your yarn needle with a length of yarn round the centre.

8. Thread one end of the yarn through a loop in your pouffe, then repeat with the other end of yarn.

9. Tie both ends of yarn together in a tight double knot to secure the pom pom in place on your pouffe. Repeat steps 7-9 until as much of the pouffe as you want is covered in pom poms. You can cover it entirely or just cover the top to show both textures!

10. Use a variety of sizes of pom pom to fill in any gaps. You want to ensure your pom poms create a thick covering on your pouffe to look really effective. Once you have stitched all of your pom poms onto the pouffe, your stool is complete!

resin art clock

I had lots of fun finding buttons and beads to use in this resin clock. The beads are from bracelets given to me by my brother that I no longer wear. They really sparkle through the glossy resin and it was great to give them a second life!

Time required:
This project takes 4 hours to make and 24 hours to cure

You will need:
- A 10" (25cm) silicon cake mould
- Variety of decorative items to dip into your mould – beads, confetti, flowers etc
- 2-part epoxy resin
- Clock movement
- Clock hands
- A drill (to make a hole in the centre of the piece to affix the clock!)
- Disposable container
- Lollipop stick
- Tweezers
- Plastic measuring cup
- AA battery
- Glitter
- Greaseproof paper

Resin can be difficult to work with but used correctly it is a brilliant material that can create some amazing results. This resin art clock looks stunning as a feature on a plain wall. You can put anything you like into the clock face itself. I love the idea of putting special memorabilia or small treasured items inside to preserve them forever.

This is the largest project in the book and you will need to follow the steps carefully to get it right, but it's worth it; I promise!

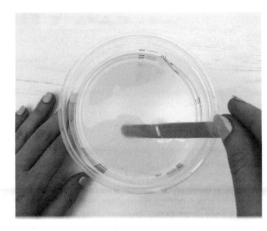

INSTRUCTIONS

1. Cover your work surface with greaseproof paper to protect it. Resin doesn't stick to greaseproof paper so this will stop your work from getting stuck.

2. Mix one ounce of your chosen resin in your disposable container, according to manufacturer's instructions. Stir continuously for at least 2 minutes, using a lollipop stick, to ensure it is evenly mixed

3. Pour a layer of resin approximately 0.5-1cm thick into your silicon cake mould. Put this to one side and allow the resin to cure slightly.

4. Once this layer has become jelly-like, you are ready to start embedding your decorative items.
5. Mix two more ounces of resin according to the packet instructions ready to use for the next steps.

6. Using tweezers, dip your decorative items into the resin and add them to your clock mould. Anything you want to be visible from the front of the clock should be placed into the mould face down.

7. Arrange your pieces carefully, using larger and smaller items to create a visually interesting effect.
8. Once you are happy with your design pour your remaining resin directly into the cake mould.

9. Mix up a further 1-2 ounces of resin. If you want to add glitter then stir it into the resin at this stage.
10. Pour the resin directly into the cake mould. Put this to one side to cure for 12 hours.

11. Once it is cured, pop the resin piece out of the mould. It is now time to dome the front of your design to give it a finished look.

12. Mix another 1-2 ounces of resin and pour this onto the front of your resin piece and leave it to cure for another 12 hours.

13. Once it has fully hardened, take a pen and mark the centre of your resin piece.
14. Using a drill with the same thickness drill bit as the clock movement, gently drill a hole through your mark.

15. Attach your clock movement and hands to the finished resin piece, following manufacturer's instructions. Adjust the hands to the correct time and insert your battery. Hang your clock on the wall!

yarn wall hanging

I don't like plain white walls; I find them a bit cold. This project is an easy and affordable way to dress up a plain white wall without having to commit to repainting. Perfect if you are renting – or just want to give a room a pop of colour!

Time required:
This project takes an afternoon to make

You will need:

■ Scissors

■ Tape measure

■ Wooden dowel in the length of your choice.

■ Ribbon

■ Yarn in a variety of colours

Decorating a blank wall can create a sense of warmth in your home and make even the coldest space feel cosy and safe. Use this wall hanging to dress up a boring space. It's your chance to use all the colours that you love and feel best reflect you and your style. Just go for it!

This is probably the easiest project in this book. It's simple to make but it really does pack a punch of vibrant colour, and will liven up any room!

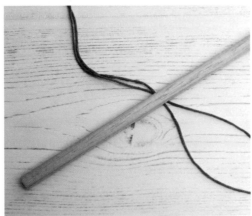

INSTRUCTIONS

1. Cut your yarn into 1.5m (60") long pieces.

2. Fold a piece of yarn in half, grab it in the middle and place it underneath the wooden dowel.

3. Grab the two ends of this piece of yarn and pull it through the loop tightly.

4. Repeat steps 1-3, changing colours when you feel like it, until the majority of the dowel is covered.

5. Knot a piece of ribbon on each end of the dowel to hang your finished piece.

6. Hang it on the wall and then trim the ends to your desired shape. I think angular shapes work best.

This is one of the easiest projects in the book, but one that I think is most effective. You need no special skills — just a good eye for colour

chapter four: gratitude makes

Being grateful and expressing your gratitude is like having a super power! It doesn't cost anything except time and you will instantly feel more satisfied and happy in your life. You will also make somebody else feel good too. The projects in this chapter were created to help you express your gratitude and to spread a bit of joy to those special people in your life through crafting. Even if that person is you, and you just need to be reminded now and again to smell the roses and enjoy living in the present.

the grateful game

Whenever I feel a bit down, I like to play 'The Grateful Game'. To play, all you have to do is to recite out loud five things big or small that you are grateful for in your life. By saying these five things out loud, you affirm to yourself how grateful you are for them. This game never fails to cheer me up no matter how bad my day is and helps me to get perspective on life.

You might be grateful for your lovely neighbour who always says hello. You might be grateful for a sunny day. You might just be grateful for the important people in your life. I believe that no matter how bad things get, there is always something in your world to be grateful for that can raise your spirits.

Being grateful for even the smallest things allows you to focus on the lighter side of life, rather than on stress and negativity. You can make the cultivation of gratitude into a habit quite easily if you play 'The Grateful Game' every day.

Another way to spread gratitude is to tell the people in your life that you are grateful for how they positively impact on your life. You will make them feel good about themselves but also give yourself a little happiness boost by making another human being smile!

This chapter of the book focuses on small makes you can do to show your gratitude to other people. I aimed to make these projects easy for you to personalise with your own messages and I kept them small so that you can also pop them in the post for those people in your life who live further afield.

We are all in this life together and by sharing a bit of gratitude we can make it happier for all of us!

clay diorama

There is something nostalgic about making something from clay. It stems back to when we were young and played with salt dough at playgroup. This project is a great excuse to unleash your inner child and create a lovely gift for a loved one.

Time required:
This project takes 4 evenings to make (including drying time)

You will need:
- Air-dry clay
- Shadow box photo frame (any size)
- E6000 glue
- Paint brushes
- Acrylic paint
- Clay sealant
- Thick coloured backing card (the same dimensions as your shadow box photo frame)
- Pencil
- Black fine liner pen
- Scissors
- Toothpick/needle (optional)
- Knife (optional)

We all have those long-distance people in our lives who rock our world! Just think of the friends you haven't spoken to for months but, when you do finally get around to catching up with them, it's like no time has passed. There are the members of your family who, even though they live far away, are always supportive and only a phone call away. These 'rock stars' are always there to support us. This project is a way to remind them how much you appreciate them despite the distance between you.

A diorama is a three-dimensional miniature model or scene and you can choose how complex you make this project depending on what you choose for your scene and how small the pieces you make are. It is suitable for beginners because you don't need to be an expert at working with clay to create a diorama; however you will need a steady hand for painting your finished clay pieces if they are very small.

This clay diorama makes a fantastic gift. You can fill it with memories and objects that are special to the person you are giving it to and they can hang it up to remind them of how much you appreciate them.

INSTRUCTIONS
1. On a flat, hard, covered surface lay out your coloured backing card. Take the inner frame of your shadow box and lay it on top of the card. Using a pencil, lightly trace around the inside of the frame on to the card. Inside this pencil rectangle is where you will glue your finished clay pieces. Put this card aside for now.

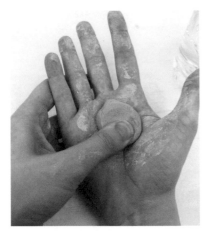

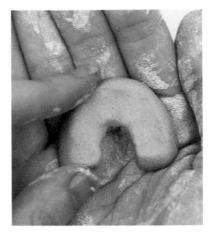

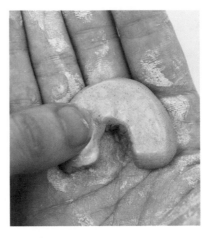

2. Time to get messy! Take your air-dry clay and cut off a small piece, making sure you store the rest of the clay in an air-tight container until you are ready to use it. Knead the clay until it is soft and pliable, adding water if it feels a bit too dry.

3. Start to shape your clay to make your pieces. You could make your friend's favourite food, a simple outline of their favourite place or even an object that refers to an inside joke that you might have together!

4. Once you have created a basic shape, use a little bit of water and your thumb to gently smooth the surface. You should aim to have no cracks or finger prints on the surface of your object. Remember you will paint the details in later so keep your shapes simple.

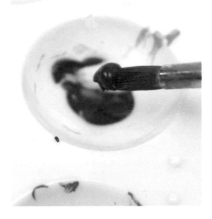

5. Aim to create between 4-6 clay shapes. You don't want to overcrowd your diorama or leave it looking too sparse. Once you have made your shapes, leave them overnight to harden and dry for at least 12 hours.

6. When the shapes are dry, it's time to paint them using acrylic paint and a small paintbrush. If you have used grey air-dry clay, firstly paint all of the shapes white so any colours will pop. Leave them to dry before moving on.

7. It's time to add the details to your shapes. When painting with acrylic paint try not to thin your paint down with too much water or it will run. Use small amounts of thicker paint for strong colours.

8. Start by painting any larger areas of your shape first. So, for example, if you are painting an animal then start by painting the main colour of their body and add any other colours on top.

9. For finer details such as faces or highlights – use a fine tipped paintbrush and carefully add these details once the main colours are dry to prevent any smudging.

10. Leave your clay shapes to dry completely. Once dry, brush a thin layer of clay sealant over each shape. This will create a nice shiny finish. Leave your shapes to dry.

11. Now it's time to glue your shapes on to the card. Make sure you glue them inside the rectangle shape you drew earlier. Lay out your design before you stick them on to ensure you are happy with your final design.

12. Next apply a small amount of E6000 glue to the back of your shapes using a toothpick and press the shapes onto the card in your chosen design. Leave it all to dry for at least 24 hours.

13. Use a fine line black pen to write some nice sentiments or messages on your diorama. This could just be a nice phrase, a joke that you share or a nickname. When finished put it in the shadow box frame ready to hang.

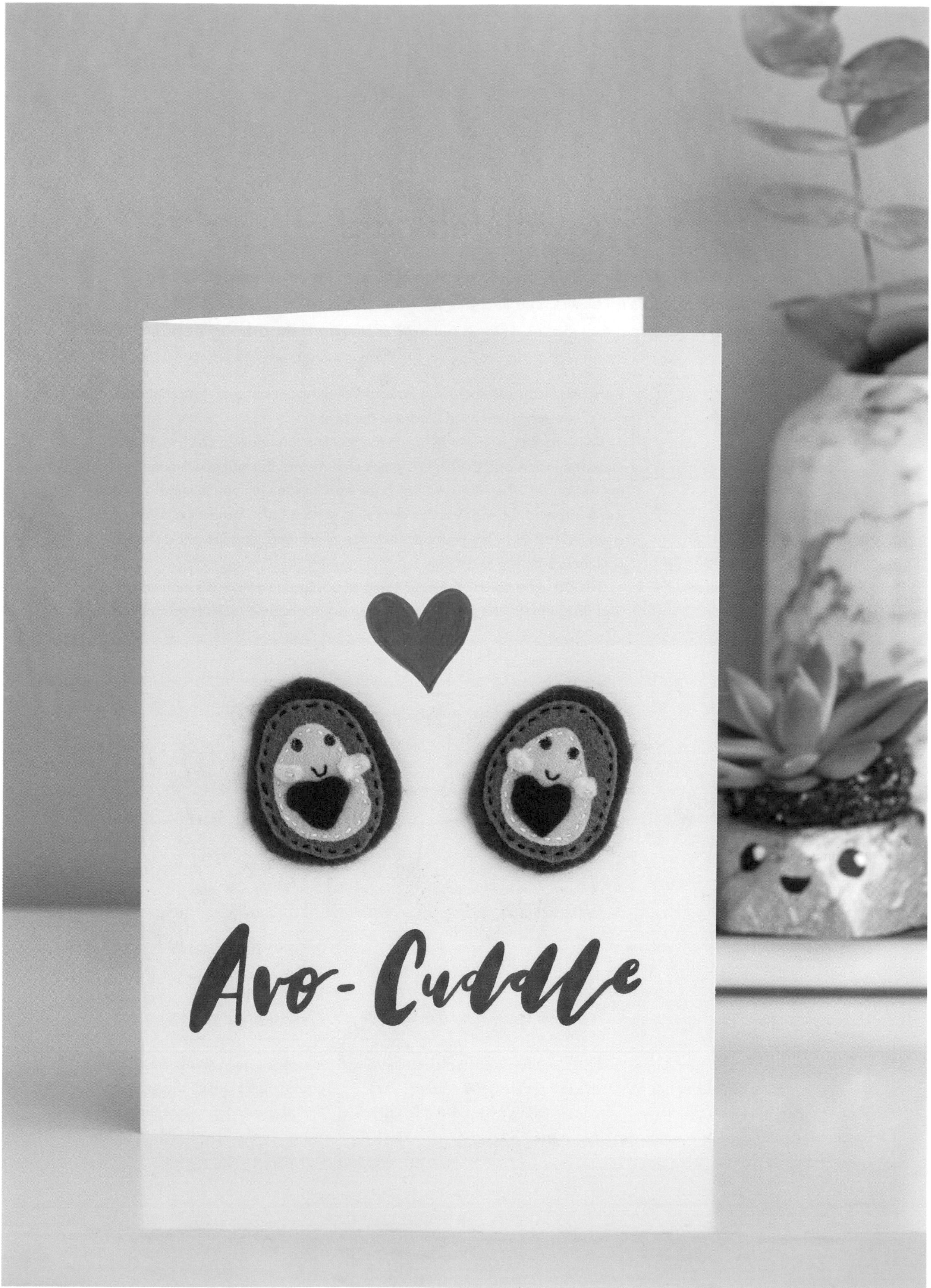
Avo-Cuddle

kawaii felt card

There is something really special about receiving a card in the post, especially one that somebody has taken the time to make for you. This cute card is beautifully tactile with a 3D effect that makes it stand out from a standard shop-bought card.

Time required:
This project takes 2 hours to make plus 2 hours drying time

You will need:
- Template (see templates chapter)
- White/coloured A4 card
- Dark green felt
- Medium green felt
- Light green felt
- Dark brown felt
- Pink felt
- Black thread
- White thread
- Stick on googly eyes (5mm size)
- PVA glue
- Black and red pens

Living in a world of social media and WhatsApp it's easy to forget about the joy that comes from receiving a card in the post.

Knowing that somebody has taken the time to choose a card, write the message inside and post it, is a great pick-me up. But that positive feeling is even stronger when the card has been handmade with you in mind! You don't need a special occasion as an excuse to send a card. Sending a card can be a way of just showing your appreciation of a friend, and life is too short to wait until their birthday to do that.

This DIY cute card is the equivalent of posting a smile! It is simple to make and doesn't take long to create. Give it a go, or come up with your own design.

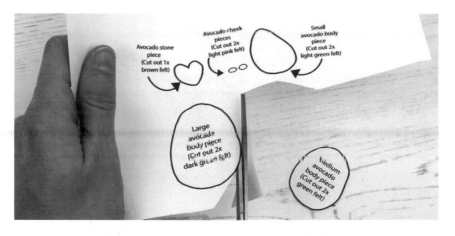

INSTRUCTIONS

1. Using the template included in this book, cut out all of the paper shapes.

2. Find the large avocado body template piece and using a black pen, draw around the template on to dark green felt. Cut out two pieces.

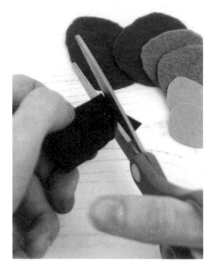

3. Cut out two pieces of the medium sized avocado body in the medium green coloured felt and put aside.

4. Then, cut out two pieces of the small avocado shape in the light green coloured felt and set aside.

5. Finally cut out one piece of the avocado pit template in your dark brown felt.

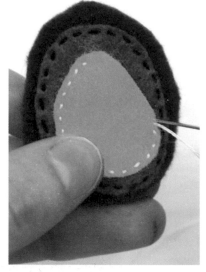

6. Stitch the medium body shape on to the larger body shape using a running stitch and the black thread. Do this twice to make two avocados.

7. Put the light green body piece on top of your stitching and, again, stitch on using running stitch and black thread. Do this twice.

8. To finish your avocado, sew the brown felt pit on to one of your avocado pieces using a small running stitch and black thread.

9. Cut out four cheek pieces in your pink felt using the template provided.

10. Using white thread, stitch two cheek pieces on each of the two avocados.

11. Using black thread and a tiny running stitch, sew a smile between the cheeks on both avocados.

12. Now put some glue on the back of the googly eyes and attach these to the avocados. Leave to dry.

13. Fold your card in half. and glue your avocados firmly on to the front of the card. Leave to dry for a few hours.

14. Using a red pen draw a heart above the two avocados and underneath, in a black pen, write the phrase 'Avo-cuddle'.

origami lucky paper stars

I first learnt how to make these when we had a Japanese exchange student to stay. I was fascinated watching her fold these tiny paper stars. Since then I have made them for friends, family and even myself when I'm procrastinating!

Time required:
These are a quick make! It will take 1-2 hours to make a full jar of lucky stars

You will need:
- Coloured/glitter A4 paper
- Scissors
- Pen
- A pretty mason jar to put them in

These lucky paper stars are so cute and make an adorable pick-me-up gift to show a friend you care. Write secret messages of support or compliments on the inside of them and give a jar of them to a friend in need. Or why not turn them into earrings, string them up to make mini bunting or just use them as decoration? They are a quick and easy make that only takes a few minutes per star. They are really addictive to make and you can write anything you like inside as a nice surprise for the recipient. Let's get making!

INSTRUCTIONS
1. Cut out a paper strip the length of a piece of portrait A4 paper and roughly 1cm wide.

2. Now write a message on this strip of paper using a black pen.

3. Fold the paper strip at an angle with the message facing down.

4. Fold the paper, with the message facing up, across the blank side. Tuck the tail behind forming a pentagon shape.

5. Wrap the paper around the pentagon shape, from side to side.

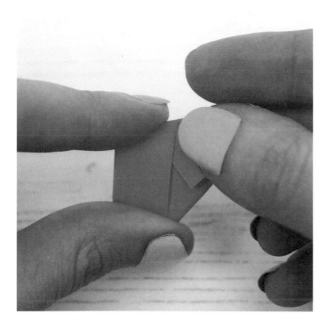

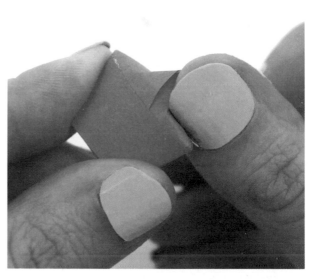

6. Tuck the remaining tail inside one of the paper folds. You should now have one neat paper pentagon.

7. With your thumb, lightly press on the middle of each side of the pentagon to cause your star to puff up!

8. Your first star might look a little bit wonky but it just takes a bit of practice to get them all evenly sized.

9. Once you have made your stars, put them in a mason jar and gift them to a special friend.

peg prompts

This simple project packs a punch. When I first thought up the idea for this I wasn't sure if I would be able to fill every peg with a message. But surprisingly I found it easy; it turns out there is a lot to be grateful for!

Time required:
This make takes between 1-4 hours to make depending on the number of pegs.

You will need:
- Wooden clothes pegs
- Acrylic paint
- Paint pen/marker pen
- Thick card circle (if you want to display your pegs as a wreath)
- Ribbon (30mm in width)

Happiness comes from appreciating what you have in the moment. On the days when you aren't feeling your best, you can use gratitude to boost your mood and remind you of all of the good things in your life.

You can use these peg prompts to hold your photos in a pretty way and as a reminder of the things in your life to be happy and grateful for. Arranging them into a colourful wreath makes an unusual and imaginative gift for a friend who maybe needs a little happiness boost. It's a simple idea but the messages can mean so much.

INSTRUCTIONS 1. On a well-covered surface, start to paint your clothes pegs using acrylic paint. I love to use bright colours for this project.

2. A mix of four colours in varying shades looks particularly effective. Leave the pegs to dry for a few hours once you've painted them.

3. Whilst the pegs are drying, get your card ready. Use a protractor or a couple of round objects to draw two concentric circles.

4. Cut out your circle so you have a ring of cardboard that is approximately 8-10cm wide.

5. When the pegs are dry, using a paint pen, start to write your messages of gratitude. They can be anything from a great TV series on Netflix to an amazing new takeaway.

6. Once your pegs are completely dry, clip them to the cardboard ring to complete the wreath.

7. Tie a loop of ribbon at the front of the middle of the wreath to hang it on the wall.

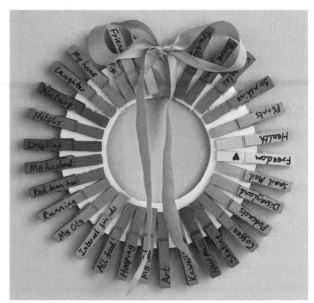

8. You can display your pegs on your wreath or use them to peg up your favourite photos or cards!

chapter five: tidy mind makes

There is nothing wrong with a little bit of mess; a bit of organised chaos. I don't know many people who are super tidy! On those days when everything seems a bit overwhelming, just knowing where your things are can help to make those mundane everyday jobs stress free and easy. The projects in this chapter will help you to stay organised and on top of the little things in life so that you can free up your mind to focus on more important things.

Tidy house tidy mind

Can I tell you a secret?

I'm messy...everywhere I go I leave a mess! My desk at home is never tidy and I am definitely the person whose idea of tidying up consists of carefully placing all of my mess into one big drawer. Out of sight out of mind, right?

It's only recently that I realised that I can't go on being this messy. It's fine when I'm feeling relaxed and happy because, despite the mess, I always seem to know where everything is. But on those days when I'm worn out and feeling stressed, trying to hunt through my disorganised drawers to find something like a specific type of yarn, it is just one thing too many and can lead me to have a bit of a meltdown.

There is definitely some truth behind the saying 'tidy house, tidy mind'. Being organised can help you to feel grounded even if the rest of your life or your emotions are in chaos. It is important not to spend any of your mental energy on worrying about where to find your belongings.

Being organised is a form of self-care. You don't need to be super tidy all of the time, (believe me my workspace is far from spotless!), but even if you just organise a few things in your life, it can help to take a weight off your mind.

In this chapter of the book I've designed projects to help you to organise some of those small annoyances in your life, like tangled jewellery and knotted headphones. So even if you are a messy monster like me, you can still organise a small part of your life. Your future self will be grateful – trust me!

macramé jewellery organiser

I'm a bit of a magpie when it comes to jewellery and I particularly love necklaces, but I don't love how they always tangle together. This simple project will make it easier to find your favourite necklace when you are in a hurry.

Time required:
This project needs 4 hours of drying time, but once dry it takes only 30 minutes to put together

You will need:

■ Teal macramé cord

■ Purple macramé cord

■ Blue macramé cord

■ Wooden dowelling in 3 different lengths – 15cm, 25cm and 35cm (6, 10 or 14") of your chosen width

■ Washi tape (in a colour of your choice)

■ Gold acrylic paint

■ D-ring

When things are getting on top of you and your mind feels cluttered, it can help to focus on the things in your life that you do have control over and forget the problems or worries that are not in your power.

One thing that you will always have control over is keeping yourself and your home organised. This is a simple project that only takes a short time to put together but it looks beautiful. It's minimalist style means that you can hang it almost anywhere in your home and it will fit in with your decor.

While you are making this jewellery organiser, just focus on the process of creating something beautiful and practical.

INSTRUCTIONS

1. On a covered surface take the washi tape and wrap it around the end of each piece of wooden dowelling just a few centimetres from the end.

2. Paint the tips of each piece of wooden dowelling with the gold acrylic paint. Leave these to dry for 2-4 hours.

3. Once the dowels are dry then you can peel off the washi tape leaving a nice neat edge.

4. Cut a length of approximately 2m of each colour of macramé cord.

5. Hold all the cord pieces together and fold them in half. Then loop them through the D-ring.

6. Pull the ends of the cord through the loop to secure them to the D-ring.

7. Take the now dry dowelling and, starting with the smallest piece, tie the cord to it.

8. Plait 30cm of one of the pieces of cord, leaving the other piece unbraided.

9. Once plaited, tie the cord on to either end of the medium piece of dowelling.

10. Tie the remaining unbraided pieces of cord to the final large piece of dowelling. Leave the ends trailing and trim them to the same length to finish.

kawaii felt taco headphone organiser

Since making this little happy taco, my tangled headphones have become a thing of the past! Made of felt, this project is an easy sewing project if you are new to sewing by hand as felt needs no complicated finishing.

Time required:
This project takes only 2 hours to make, so it's the perfect make for sitting in front of the TV one evening

You will need:
- Pink felt
- Yellow felt
- Green felt
- Red felt
- Brown felt
- Yellow, black and pink cotton thread
- Scissors
- Sewing needle
- 1 small snap fastening
- Pins
- Template (see templates chapter)
- Pencil

One of life's little annoyances is opening your bag to pull out your headphones, to find them in a big tangled mess.

With this cute little DIY you can stop the problem and it will make you smile every time you use it!

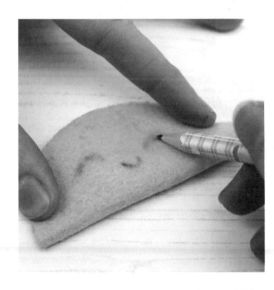

INSTRUCTIONS

1. On a flat work surface, cut out all of the paper template pieces. Following the instructions on the templates, draw round them on to the corresponding pieces of felt, and cut out the felt shapes. You might need two pieces for certain shapes – check the template to see. Put one of the yellow circles of felt on to your work surface.

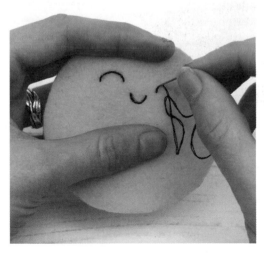

2. Now add the face. Using a pencil, carefully draw two arches as eyes and a small U-shape for the mouth. Thread your needle with black thread (if you are using embroidery thread, use 2 strands for this) and carefully stitch along the pencil lines Tie a knot to finish off your sewing.

3. Using the eyes as a guide, place the pink felt cheek pieces slightly below and to the side of each eye and sew on with pink thread and a small running stitch, or use fabric glue if you don't like sewing.

4. Turn the yellow felt circle face side down and lay the brown felt on top. Make sure that some of the brown felt sticks out over the edge of the yellow felt.

5. Next, place the red felt on top of the brown felt.
6. Finally take the pieces of green felt, and lay them on top of the red, yellow and brown felts as shown. Carefully place this to one side.

7. Take the second circle of yellow felt and using yellow thread carefully stitch the snap fastenings to the felt circle. There should be one fastening at the top and one fastening directly underneath.

8. Place the felt circle with the fastenings on top of the felt taco that you put to one side earlier with the fastenings face up.

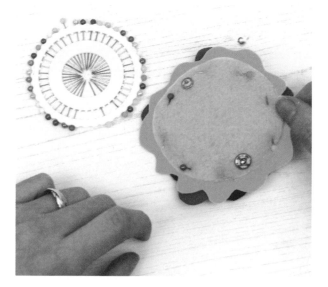

9. Being careful not to move the filling too much, pin the two sides of the taco together, trapping the felt fillings inside.

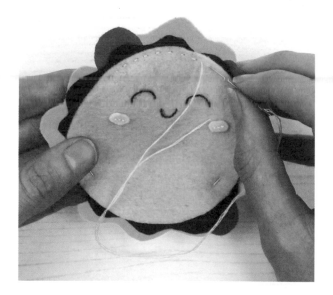

10. Thread your needle, and using a tiny running stitch, carefully stitch around the edges of the two pieces of yellow felt. Tie a knot in the thread to secure.

11. Your taco is now complete! You can wrap your headphones around the middle so that they never get tangled again!

kawaii toast make-up bag

Kawaii is Japanese for cute and typically features characters with large eyes and small smiles to make them even cuter! I love the aesthetic. This make-up bag is cute but practical and designed to make you smile every time you use it.

Time required:

This project takes approximately one afternoon to stitch – it can be stitched by hand or on a sewing machine if you want to complete it even faster.

You will need:

- ■ Template (see templates chapter)
- ■ Zip 18cm (7") long
- ■ Scissors
- ■ Sewing needle
- ■ Chalk
- ■ Light brown, white, and black cotton threads
- ■ Yellow felt
- ■ Pink felt
- ■ Black felt
- ■ White felt
- ■ Light brown plush
- ■ Dark brown plush 20x45cm (8"x8")
- ■ Lining fabric 20x45cm (8"x8")
- ■ Pins

Who doesn't love toast? It's warm, comforting and simple. It always reminds me of cold winter evenings and lazy Sunday mornings!

This little bag is useful for keeping your make-up or any other bits and bobs all together. It's a bit trickier than some of the other projects in this book because you have to learn how to attach a zip. Having said that, it's definitely possible for a beginner to stitch with some patience.

Hopefully this cute make-up bag will give you a comforting feeling on those days when you need it most!

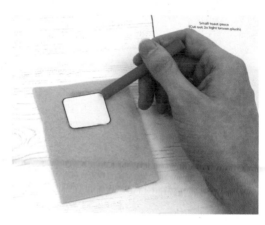

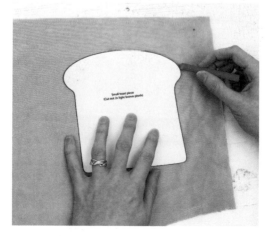

INSTRUCTIONS

1. On a flat surface cut out all of the paper templates.

2. Check the instructions written on the templates to see which colour felt to use for each piece. Draw round the templates using chalk and cut out your felt pieces and put them on one side.

3. Take the light brown plush fabric and place it plush side down. Draw around the paper template using chalk and cut out your toast shape. Cut out two pieces and put them to one side.

107

4. Cut out the light brown plush and lining fabrics using the largest paper template.

5. When cutting out these templates, leave a seam allowance of roughly 1cm (½").

6. Take one of the light brown plush fabric pieces and place it on a flat surface, plush side facing up.

7. Arrange the eyes, eye highlights, smile, cheeks and butter felt pieces on the light brown plush and pin them on ready to sew.

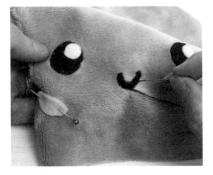

8. Carefully stitch the felt pieces into place using a neat running stitch and the corresponding thread colour.

9. Place both pieces of dark brown plush onto a flat surface, plush side up. Pin your toast face and the other plain piece of light brown plush into place.

10. Using a neat running stitch carefully attach the light brown plush pieces to the dark brown plush fabric.

11. The next step is to insert the zip. Centre the zip on the bottom edge teeth side down and the zip pulled to the left. Pin the zip in place.

12. Carefully stitch a running stitch along the top of the zip, attaching it to the dark brown plush fabric.

13. Now place the lining pattern side down on top of the pieces that you have just sewn. Pin this into place.

14. Sew along the same zip edge, using a neat running stitch to create a zip lining sandwich, with the zip as the filling.

15. Using an iron on a low heat setting, carefully press the sewn edge away from the zip, being careful not to iron the zip teeth.

16. Stitch along the same edge a few millimetres away from the zip itself to prevent any fabric from getting caught in the zip.

17. Repeat steps 11-16 to complete the second side of the zip. Now open the zip at least halfway. This is very important!

18. Place the brown plush pieces right side together and pin them into place. Do the same for the lining pieces.

19. Stitch running stitch around the entire toast bag using a 1cm (½") seam allowance. Leave an 8cm (3") opening to turn the bag out.

20. Now comes the exciting bit! Place your hand into the opening you left in the lining and turn your bag right side out.

21. Pull the lining out and gently stitch the opening with a running stitch. Put the lining back into your bag and zip it up to finish.

chapter six: self-care crafting

Self-care is all about spending the time on ourselves that we need to be our best. It's not selfish to take a moment for yourself. It will ensure your mental wellness in the long term. Self-care comes in all shapes and sizes, from small day-to-day moments such as doing a face mask in the evening to bigger moments of self care such as having a day away from social media. The projects in this chapter are both relaxing to make and also will serve as a reminder to allow yourself some self-care moments. You deserve it.

make time for you

This world is so busy and it's all go, go, go! It can be tricky to make time for yourself without feeling guilty for doing so. Social media has a lot to answer for!

The phrase self-care gets thrown about a lot these days. But what does it actually mean?

Self-care consists of all the things you do to take of yourself to protect your mental well-being. It isn't about doing specific activities; it is about doing what is right for you in order to ensure your mental wellness.

Self-care can take many forms. Personally, I like to turn off my phone and step away from the screen. Then I like to go for a run, do some knitting, cross stitching and then bake something delicious. Other friends of mine like to lie on the sofa and read a book or spend an evening putting on a face mask. I am somebody who is really bad at sitting still so this form of self-care wouldn't work for me, but it works for them! Self-care is all about doing what suits you personally and makes you feel good.

Remembering to make time for self-care can sometimes be half of the battle. So, this chapter of the book contains a mixture of makes that are both relaxing and can be used as a reminder for future self-care moments.

Because after all what is more deserving of our time than a moment to care for our mental health?

Make Things Happen!

embroidery patch

I first started learning embroidery when I was 22 so I was a relative late comer, but I have been hooked ever since. This patch is a great beginner embroidery project because it only uses two different stitches that are easy to master.

Time required:
This project takes roughly 3-4 evenings to make

You will need:
- Transfer paper
- Iron and ironing board
- White cotton fabric 20x20cm (8"x8")
- Embroidery thread in colours of your choice
- Template (see templates chapter)
- Embroidery hoop 13cm (5")
- Iron on interfacing
- Embroidery scissors

The most important thing in the world is to be yourself and to be confident enough to show the world who you truly are. Expressing yourself can come in many different forms. Sometimes you don't need to speak loudly to be heard; it can be as simple as accessorising your clothing.

This patch is quick to stitch and a small way to express yourself even on the days when you might be lacking in confidence. Despite its complicated appearance, embroidery is actually a great craft for beginners. The final makes look beautiful and intricate but embroidery can actually be almost as simple as colouring in with thread.

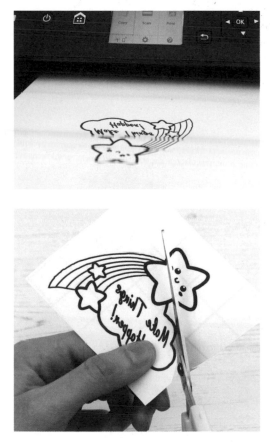

INSTRUCTIONS

1. To start, you will need to attach the design to your fabric. You can trace the design with a fabric pen on our fabric, but you might lose some detail in your lettering. Because this design is quite intricate, I recommend using transfer paper. Start by photocopying the template in this book onto your transfer paper.

2. Cut around the design as neatly as you can, trying not to leave a large border around the edge.

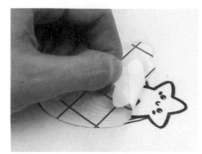

3. Put your white cotton fabric on the ironing board and following manufacturer's instructions, use an iron to gently press onto the back. Peel the backing paper.

4. You are now ready to place your fabric into your embroidery hoop, following the instructions in the basics chapter of this book.

5. Separate the strands in your thread and thread your needle, tying a small knot in the end. You are ready to start embroidering!

6. You can use a variety of different stitches to complete your patch. For larger areas such as the cloud and the star, satin stitch can be a great way to flood spaces with colour.

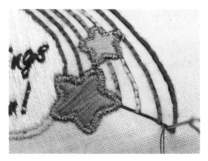

7. For any finer details, backstitch is ideal. You can also use backstitch for edges like the edges of the rainbow to give the blocks of colour better definition.

8. Backstitch is also great for lettering because it is a fine and detailed stitch. Use it for joined up letters and the smile on the star!

9. Once you're done, finish the thread by passing the needle under three of the completed stitches on the back of the fabric.

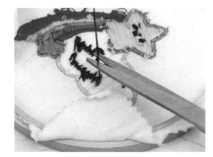

10. You can now trim the remaining thread, being very careful not to cut it too close to the fabric or it will unravel.

11. Once you have completed the embroidery patch it's time to attach it to your clothing. First remove the fabric from the hoop.

12. Take your embroidery scissors and gently trim around the edge of your patch. Cut as close to your stitches are possible, but be careful not to cut through them.

13. You now have a finished patch. Congratulations! Place your patch on your iron-on interfacing face down and trace around it.

14. Cut out the interfacing.

15. Place your patch face down on an ironing board then place the interfacing on top of the back of the patch, textured side down.

16. Using an iron on the heat setting recommended in your interfacing instructions, gently apply even pressure to the interfacing. Remove the heat.

17. Once cooled, gently peel off the backing of the interfacing.

18. Place the patch on a piece of clothing. Place a piece of baking paper on the front of the patch to protect it and apply even pressure with the iron. This will fuse your patch to your clothing.

'you are enough' felt banner

Sometimes we need to be our own cheerleader and that's what this project is all about. If you can sew a simple running stitch then you will be able to make this banner easily. Hang it where you will see it everyday and make it your mantra.

Time required:
This project takes an afternoon to complete

You will need:
- Template (see templates chapter)
- A variety of coloured felt
- Canvas fabric 0.5m x 0.5m (20"x20")
- Wooden dowelling 35cm (14") in length and 1cm (½") thick
- Ribbon/yarn to hang the banner
- Embroidery thread in colours to match the felt
- Sewing needle
- Scissors
- Fabric chalk/pencil/ light coloured pen
- Pins (optional)

If you are looking for a project that will take just an afternoon to complete, then this hand-stitched felt banner is the perfect make for you. It is very simple to stitch and requires only a few materials to make. If you like, you can even use leftover scraps of fabric instead of felt. You can also use the techniques to create your own design of banner.

Once completed you can hang it on your wall and admire the cute design whilst reminding yourself that, despite all of the pressures and expectations of modern life, you are enough!

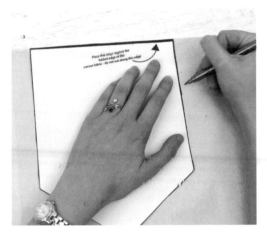

INSTRUCTIONS
1. Cut out the banner, heart and letter templates. Fold the canvas fabric in half and place your template on the folded edge. Draw around the template.

2. Cut out the canvas fabric, remembering not to cut along the folded edge of the material.

4. Put this canvas piece to one side. Place the lettering and heart paper templates on your chosen felt and trace around them.

5. Cut out all of these felt pieces carefully using sharp scissors to make sure the shapes are crisp.

6. Unfold your canvas fabric piece and, using the photo of the finished banner as a guide, pin your felt pieces on one side of your fabric.

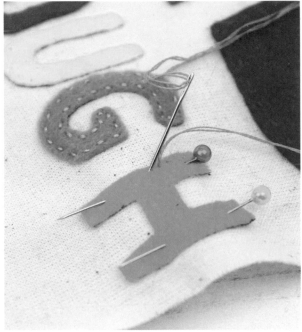

7. Thread a sewing needle with the colour of embroidery thread that matches your felt.

8. Stitch the felt piece into place using tiny running stitches around the edge of the piece. Do this for all of the felt pieces.

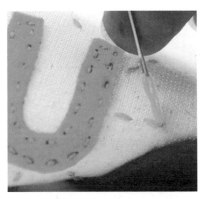

9. Using a pencil or light coloured pen carefully mark the face details on to the heart felt shape.

10. Carefully backstitch along these marks using two strands of black embroidery thread.

11. You can add other embroidery details. I added backstitching around the edge of the letters for some added definition but this isn't strictly necessary; you could leave your banner as it is and move straight to the next step.

12. Fold the canvas fabric back in half and, using running stitch, carefully sew both the folded pieces together. Be sure to leave a 2cm gap at the top of your banner for your wooden dowelling.

13. Slide the wooden dowelling into the banner and tie a length of ribbon or yarn on to both ends of it. Your banner is now ready to hang up!

kawaii tassel necklace

I had lots of fun making tassels for this project. When I first learnt how to make tassels I was amazed at how easy they are to make, but yet they look so effective and can add so much personality to an outfit. I knew I had to include them!

Time required:
This project takes 2 hours to make and 24 hours to dry

You will need:
- Embroidery thread in a variety of colours
- Scissors
- Chain with a clasp already attached
- Gemstone silicon mould
- Cement
- Jump ring x 2
- E6000 Glue
- Fold over crimp x 1
- Water
- Throw away bowl
- Lollipop stick
- Scissors
- Needle nose pliers
- Vaseline
- Pencil
- Acrylic paint
- Varnish

Cement is a beautifully tactile material. When it's wet, it's messy and squidgy and when it hardens it has a ridged surface that is hard to resist running your hands over.

This necklace combines the softness of flowing tassels with the hardness of the cement pendant. It's a messy make, but it is worth it. Just make sure you put down lots of newspaper to protect your surfaces first.

Jewellery is a small way that you can express yourself confidently, whilst bringing a bit of your personality to an outfit. It's a tiny act of rainbow rebellion against dull office wear!

INSTRUCTIONS

1. Make sure all of your surfaces are covered before you start to mix up your cement. It can get messy!

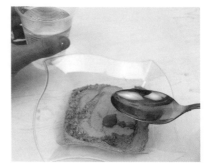

2. Put a small amount of cement mix into the container and add water in small increments, stirring the mixture as you go.

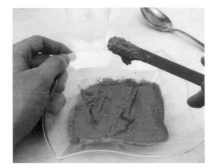

3. Once you have a consistency that is similar to thick soup then stop adding more water.

4. Rub a thin layer of Vaseline into your gemstone mould.

5. Pour in enough cement to fill your chosen shape for the pendant. Leave to dry for 12-24 hours.

6. You will know when the concrete is dry as it will start to come away from the edge of the mould. Take it out of the mould.

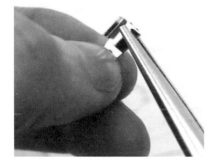

7. Using your needle nose pliers and a flat surface flatten down each side of your folding crimp.

8. Using a tiny blob of the E6000 glue, attach the folding crimp to the back of your pendant. Leave to dry for 2 hours.

9. You can now paint your pendant. I painted mine with a gold paint, but you can just apply a light varnish or omit this step.

10. Attach your pendant to your necklace chain using the folding crimp loop and your pliers.

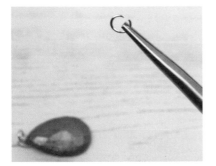

11. Now take your second jump ring and open it up with the pliers.

12. Attach the loop of the first jump ring onto the second so that your pendant is now attached to the second jump ring.

13. Before closing the jump ring ensure your necklace chain is in the middle of the ring and then close it using your pliers.

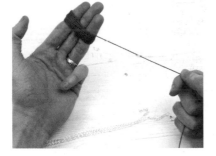

14. Time to add tassels. Wrap your embroidery thread around three of your fingers 15 to 20 times.

15. The more times you wind it around your fingers the thicker the tassel will be. When you've finished, snip off excess thread

16. Carefully ease the tassel off your finger and onto a pencil, making sure it doesn't unravel in the process.

17. Wrap a small piece of the same coloured thread around the tassel near the pencil. Secure with a double knot.

18. Thread the tassel onto your necklace. Once it's in position, tighten the tassel by pushing the knot towards the chain.

19. Cut through the bottom loop of the tassel to separate the strands. Now simply add as many tassels as you like until it's finished.

chapter seven: hibernate

Staying in is the new going out! Sometimes just having an evening in can be the recharge that you need to see out the rest of the week. Catch up on your favourite TV show, call an old friend, get immersed in a good book that you have always wanted to read. Staying in allows you to go slow, take stock and take some time out. This chapter is full of cosy snuggly projects that are perfect for shutting the world out when you need to. Because it's okay to step away for a while if that's what you need.

recharge your mind

I used to be really bad at saying no to those obligatory after work do's, when really all I wanted to do was to curl up on the sofa with my husband and watch some trashy TV.

The fear of missing out is real. However, sometimes it's much more important to say no and just stay in and relax, than to drag yourself out for yet another evening of serious conversation with work colleagues.

By staying in you don't have to be missing out. Instead you are choosing to spend time relaxing and doing the things that you want to do. There isn't a right or wrong way to spend your free time – as long as you are happy with the choice that you have made. So, spend that evening in guilt free and enjoy it!

A great way to recharge your batteries is by simply staying in, switching off your phone and logging off emails and social media (it's still going to be there when you get back!). By switching off it gives you time to reflect upon your day and to relax and find a bit of peace, at least for a bit. For those days and evenings when you don't want to face anybody and you want to just hibernate at home, this chapter of the book is for you. I wanted to design a variety of makes that will make your evenings in extra comfy and colourful! Step away from the world for an evening and snuggle up somewhere. These makes will help you to turn your home into a snuggle sanctuary that you can hide in – at least for a couple of hours anyway!

We all have those days when we want to shut the world out, and that's okay.

heated hand warmers

My poor circulation means that I constantly have cold hands and feet, so hand warmers like these are essential. The embroidery gives them a lovely tactile feel; you can't help but want to hold these little cats in your hands.

There is nothing more comforting than cuddling up with something warm. This little hand warmer is easy to make and can be reheated simply by just popping it in the microwave for 2 minutes.

On those days when you don't want to leave the house this hand warmer is perfect for providing a calming warmth and on cold days it's pocket sized so you can take it with you to keep cosy and warm!

Time required:
This project takes roughly 3-4 evenings to make.

You will need:
- Transfer paper
- Iron and ironing board
- White cotton fabric 20x20cm (8"x8")
- Embroidery thread in colours of your choice
- Dried rice or barley
- Template (see templates chapter)
- Embroidery hoop 13x13cm (5")
- Iron on interfacing
- Embroidery scissors

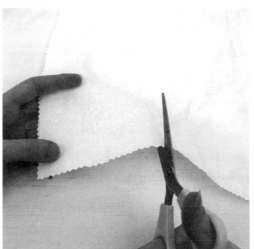

INSTRUCTIONS

1. Transfer the hand warmer designs on to your fabric. Because the designs are quite intricate. I recommend photocopying your template on to transfer paper. If you don't want to use transfer paper, you can trace the designs with a fabric pen but you might lose some detail.

2. Cut around the two designs as neatly as you can, trying not to leave too large a border around the edge.

3. Cut your cotton fabric into two equal square sized pieces bigger than your embroidery hoop.

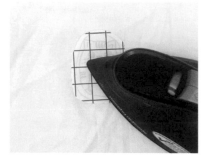

4. Transfer the design on to the centre of your fabric using a hot iron according to manufacturer's instructions for your transfer paper.

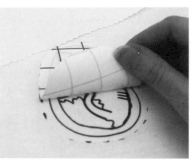

5. Carefully peel the backing paper off the design to reveal the images transferred on to your fabric.

6. Now place the first design into your embroidery hoop following instructions in the basics chapter.

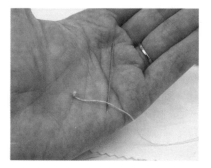

7. Separate the strands in your thread and thread your needle. Tie a small knot at the end of your thread to secure it.

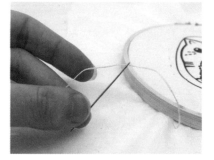

8. Now that your hoop is set up, you are ready to start embroidering! Refer to the stitch guide in the basics chapter.

9. You can use a variety of stitches to complete your hand warmer. For larger areas, such as the body and nose, satin stitch floods your design with colour.

10. Backstitch is good for any finer details or the edges of larger coloured areas like the nose, giving definition to the satin stitch.

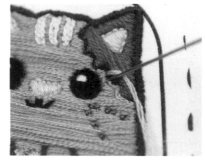

11. Backstitch is also great for facial features, because you can use it to carefully define small detailed areas such as the smile.

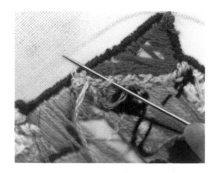

12. Once you have finished stitching you are ready to tie off your thread under the fabric.

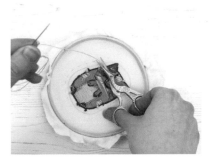

13. You can now trim the remaining thread, but be careful not to cut it too close to the fabric!

14. Remove the fabric from your hoop and repeat the process with your second piece – embroidering details and filling it in with colour.

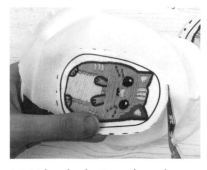

15. When both pieces have been embroidered, trim around each hand warmer piece leaving a 3cm gap/seam allowance.

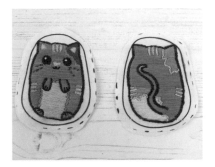

16. Place each of your embroidered pieces embroidery side up on a flat surface.

17. Place one piece on top of the other so that the embroidery sides are facing each other and pin the two pieces together.

18. Thread a needle with white thread. Using running stitch, sew the two pieces together along the edge of your seam allowance, leaving a 3cm gap.

19. Using a pencil, turn the fabric inside out through the gap, so that the embroidered pieces are now on the outside.

20. Carefully fill the fabric with dried rice or barley. You can add some drops of essential oil too if you wish (just don't over stuff it).

21. Fold in the edges of the gap and then stitch a neat running stitch along the edge. Microwave for two minutes to heat them up.

honeycomb quilted cushion

I always wanted to make a patchwork quilt when I was younger but I would always give up halfway through. My love of patchwork is what inspired this project, but it is on a smaller scale so I managed to finish it!

Time required:
This is a long-term project and takes a few weeks to make

You will need:
- Lots of fabric fat quarters in a mix of colours and patterns
- Template (see templates chapter)
- White cotton thread
- Sewing needle
- Scissors
- 50x50mm (20x20") cushion pad
- 1.5m (60") pom pom trim
- 1m (40") of plush or cotton fabric

This beautiful quilted cushion might take a little bit longer to complete than some of the other projects in this book but, once it's done, I'm sure you will agree that this was time well spent.

This project is easy to pick up and put down so you can fit it into a busy lifestyle. Just spend a few minutes every day stitching a few hexagons and before you know it you will have made this lovely rainbow cushion. You will learn how to paper pattern piece and discover how relaxing it is to rhythmically stitch these little hexagons!

INSTRUCTIONS

1. Photocopy or scan the template provided and print out several copies – you will be using a lot of paper hexagons for this project.

2. Cut out the hexagon templates.

3. Cut out your fabric shapes using your hexagon paper templates.

4. Pin the paper hexagon to your fabric, then cut around it leaving a 1.5cm (6") border around the edge.

5. Thread your needle and fold the edges of the fabric over the paper. Sew through both the paper and fabric layers.

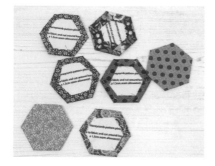

6. Your stitching doesn't need to be neat as they will not be visible later. Repeat steps 3-5 until you have several hexagon fabric pieces.

7. To start the patchwork design, pinch two of your hexagon shapes together with right sides facing each other.

8. Whip stitch the edges together, using small stitches across the fabric. Your sewing needle should go straight across your two patchwork hexagon pieces.

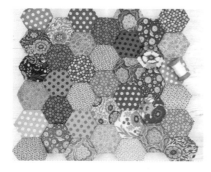

9. Keep working your way around the hexagon pieces stitching them together in any configuration that you like!

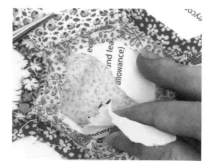

10. Remove the paper inside each template and press all of the hexagons with an iron.

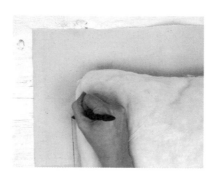

11. To make the cushion, put the pad on your chosen cushion fabric and carefully draw around it.

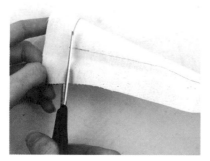

12. Cut out two pieces of fabric, leaving a 5cm (2") seam allowance around the edge of your fabric.

13. Place one piece right side up on a flat surface and pin your hexagon pieces on top.

14. Using a small running stitch sew around the edges of the patchwork attaching it to your cushion fabric.

15. Once you have attached your hexagon pieces to the front of your fabric. Lay this patchwork side face up on a flat surface.

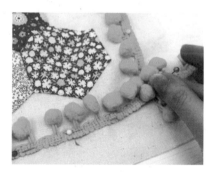

16. Cut the pom pom trim into four equal lengths of 52cm (21") and pin these to each side of the fabric with the pom poms facing inwards leaving a 5cm (2") seam.

17. Using a wide running stitch, stitch the pom pom trim onto the fabric to hold it in place when you then stitch the back piece of fabric to your cushion.

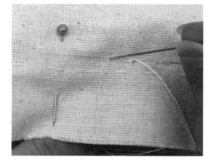

18. Place the other fabric piece on top (right side down) and pin the two pieces together with the pom poms inside. Stitch together through both layers of fabric.

19. Now for the exciting bit! Turn your cushion the right way out!

20. Fold your cushion pad in half and insert it through the gap that you left in your stitching.

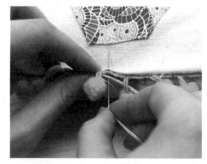

21. Fold over the edges of the gap and stitch them together neatly making sure the pom poms face out and you are done!

eye mask

I had lots of fun stitching the eyes on to this mask. It really bought it to life. You don't have to follow my design for this project; feel free to use your new embroidery skills to create your own unique design.

Time required:

This eye mask takes an afternoon to make

You will need:

- Colourful cotton fabric 30x30cm (12"x12")

- Wadding 30x30cm (12"x12")

- Plain cotton fabric 30x30cm (12"x12")

- Black embroidery thread

- Colourful elastic (that fits around your head approx 1cm (½") wide.

- Template (see templates chapter)

- Needle

- Scissors

- Cotton thread

- Chalk

- Pins (optional)

There is something indulgent about putting an eye mask on at the end of the day. It feels like a little taste of luxury. When you are anxious late at night with racing thoughts it can sometimes be difficult to relax and go to sleep. I find that an eye mask can really help. It envelopes you in darkness and can create a sense of calm. Its also great for flights and train journeys, or if you have a partner who likes to read late into the night!

This little eye mask is super cute and easy peasy to stitch up!

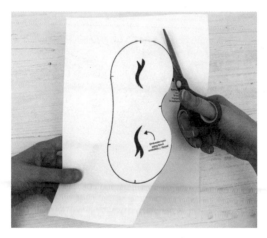

INSTRUCTIONS

1. Cut out the paper template.

2. Draw around this template and cut out 1 pattern piece from the colourful cotton fabric, 1 pattern piece from the plain fabric and 1 pattern piece from the wadding. Leave a 1cm (½") seam allowance around each piece.

3. Trim round the edges of the wadding by 1.5cm (½") so it will fit in between the other two fabric pieces later.

4. Measure the elastic by placing it around your head and then cutting it to size. You don't want it to be too tight or too loose.

5. Place the colourful cotton fabric piece colourful side up. This will be the front piece of your eye mask.

6. Take a piece of chalk and on the front of the mask mark out two upside down U shapes! Use the template eye shapes as a guide.

7. Thread your needle with 4 strands of black embroidery thread, and carefully backstitch over the lines. Fill in with satin stitch.

8. Once you have finished stitching, tie a small knot in your thread and trim off any excess.

9. Place the embroidered fabric embroidery side down on a flat surface.

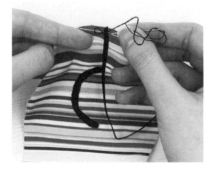

10. With a 1cm (½") seam allowance attach the elastic to the fabric using a neat running stitch.

11. Lay the plain fabric piece on top of the piece with the elastic attached and pin these two pieces together.

12. Stitch around the edges of the eye mask using a neat running stitch, leaving a 1.5cm (½") seam allowance. Leave a 10cm (4") gap at the top of the eye mask. This is really important as it

allows the wadding to be pushed into place later on. Snip small triangle notches around the seam allowance every 2.5cm (1"). Be very careful not to snip through the stitching.

13. Turn your eye mask inside out through the gap that you have left.
14. Slip the wadding into the eye mask through the gap and smooth it out using your fingers.

15. Fold the seam allowances inside the gap and pin it closed.

16. Stitch tiny running stitches to close the gap. Wear your new adorable eye mask with pride!

TEMPLATE INFORMATION

For several of the projects in this book you will require a template. Each template unless stated is true to size for the project. If you wish to increase or decrease the size of any of the projects then you can always scan them or use a photocopier to alter their size. Please note that whilst these templates and patterns are free for your personal use, these templates and patterns are copyrighted and not to be used in a commercial capacity, for instance, to make goods for sale or to sell the template themselves.

Daily ritual embroidery abstract shape template Page 18
Print this template on to transfer paper and iron it on to your fabric

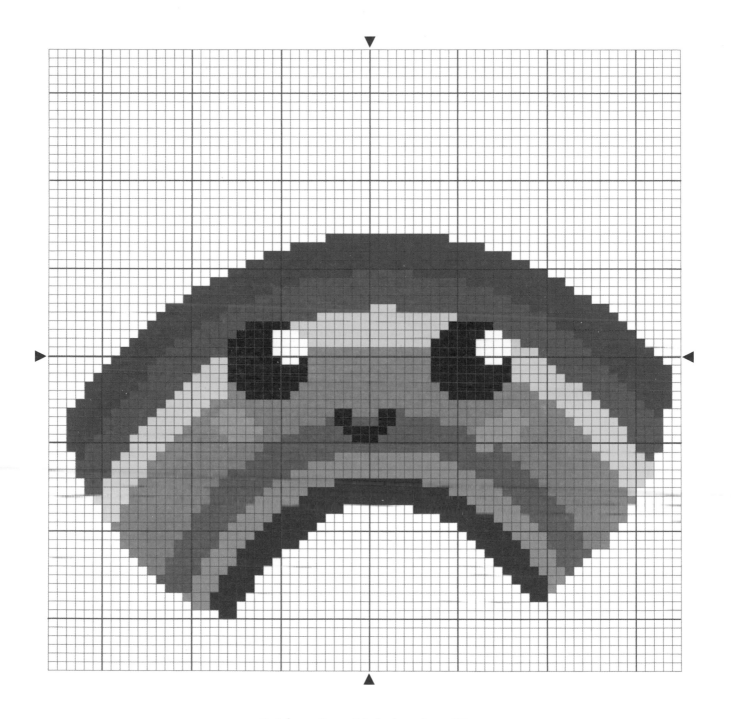

Rainbow Cross Stitch chart Page 30
Each coloured square in this template represents a single cross stitch. Start from the centre of
this pattern and colour in each square as you go – so that you don't lose your way!

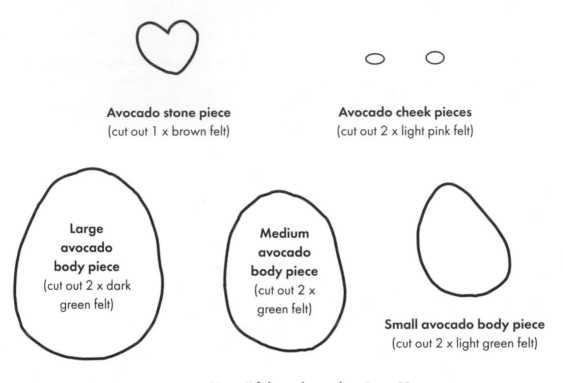

Avocado stone piece
(cut out 1 x brown felt)

Avocado cheek pieces
(cut out 2 x light pink felt)

Large avocado body piece
(cut out 2 x dark green felt)

Medium avocado body piece
(cut out 2 x green felt)

Small avocado body piece
(cut out 2 x light green felt)

Kawaii felt card template Page 82

Embroidery patch template Page 114
Print this template on to transfer paper and iron it on your fabric

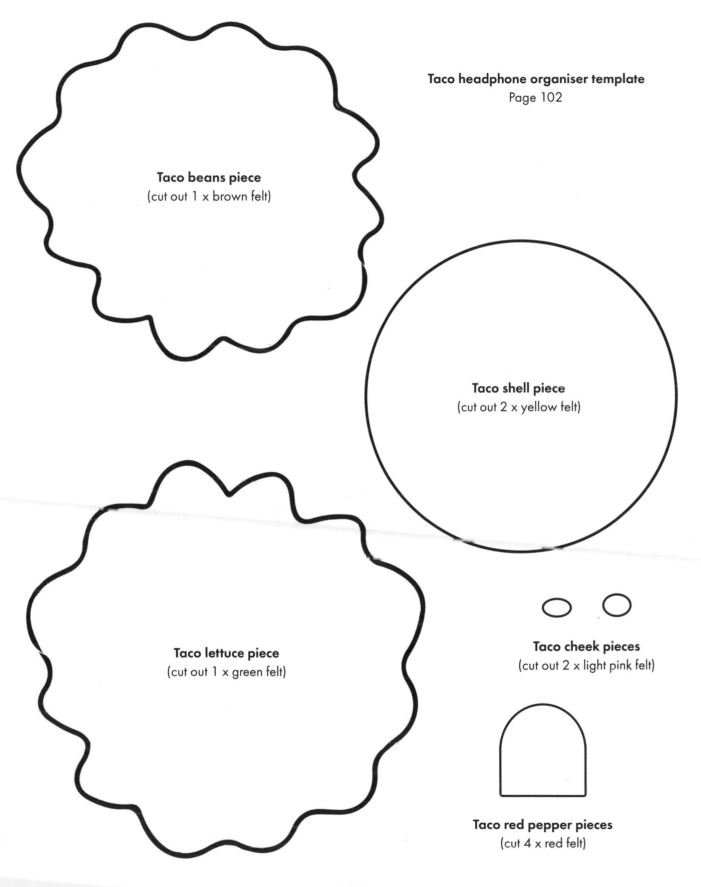

Taco headphone organiser template
Page 102

Taco beans piece
(cut out 1 x brown felt)

Taco shell piece
(cut out 2 x yellow felt)

Taco lettuce piece
(cut out 1 x green felt)

Taco cheek pieces
(cut out 2 x light pink felt)

Taco red pepper pieces
(cut 4 x red felt)

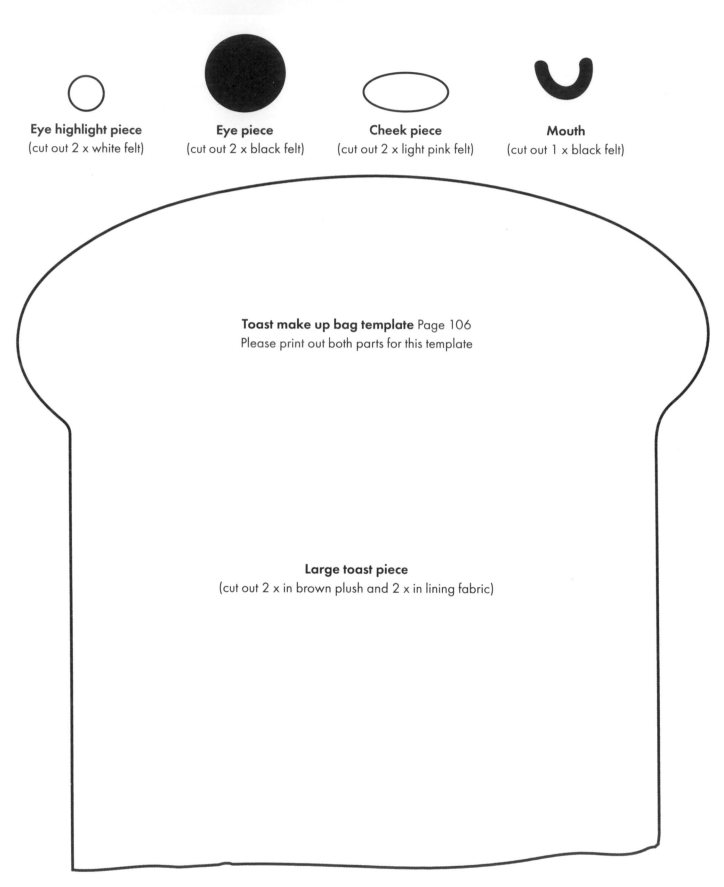

Eye highlight piece
(cut out 2 x white felt)

Eye piece
(cut out 2 x black felt)

Cheek piece
(cut out 2 x light pink felt)

Mouth
(cut out 1 x black felt)

Toast make up bag template Page 106
Please print out both parts for this template

Large toast piece
(cut out 2 x in brown plush and 2 x in lining fabric)

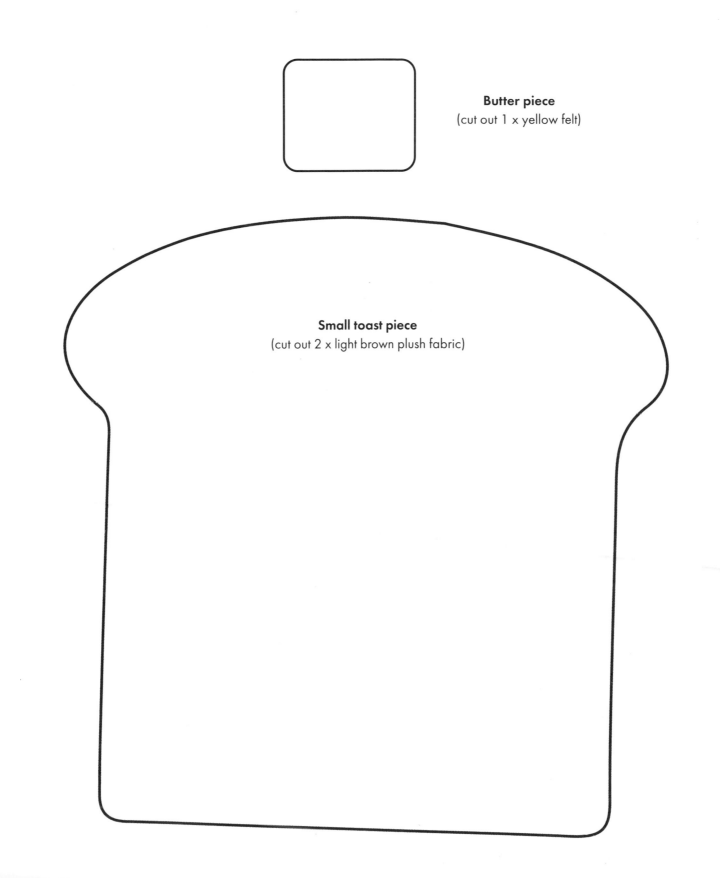

Butter piece
(cut out 1 x yellow felt)

Small toast piece
(cut out 2 x light brown plush fabric)

Lettering pieces
(cut out 1 x each letter in your choice of felt colour)

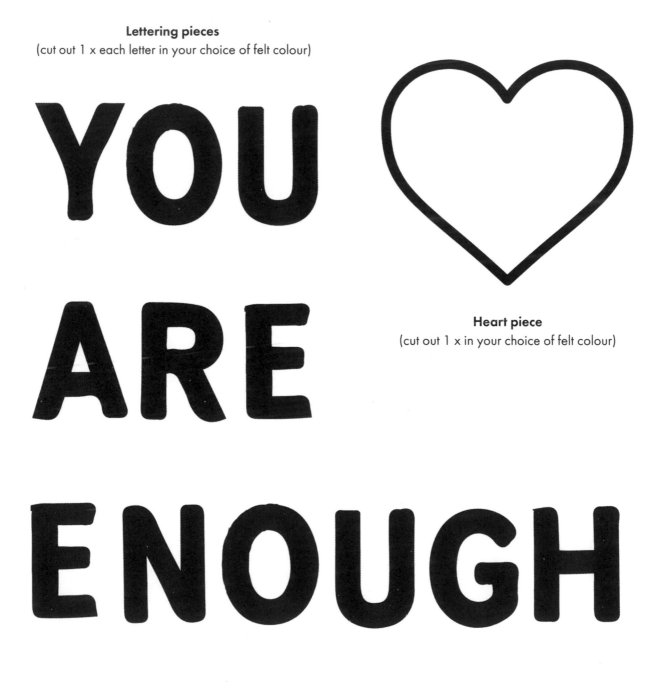

Heart piece
(cut out 1 x in your choice of felt colour)

Felt banner template Page 118
Please print out both parts for this template.

Place this edge against the folded edge of the canvas fabric – do not cut along this edge

Banner piece
(cut out 1 x canvas fabric)

Hand warmer front piece (cut out 2 x pieces)
Cut along the dotted line to leave a seam allowance.
Then stitch back and front together along the solid line
(once embroidered)

Hand warmer back piece (cut out 2 x pieces)
Cut along the dotted line to leave a seam allowance.
Then stitch back and front together along the solid line
(once embroidered)

Cat hand warmer template Page 130. Print out two of this template onto transfer paper and iron them onto your fabric.

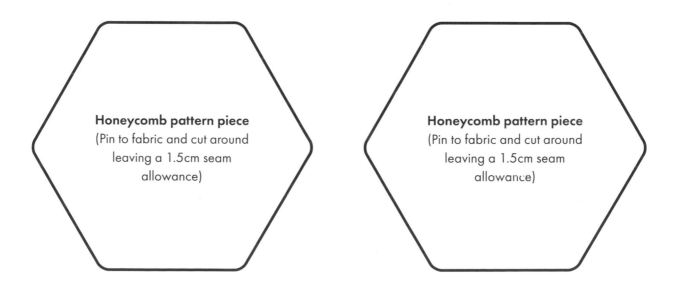

Honeycomb pattern piece
(Pin to fabric and cut around
leaving a 1.5cm seam
allowance)

Honeycomb pattern piece
(Pin to fabric and cut around
leaving a 1.5cm seam
allowance)

Honeycomb quilting cushion template Page 134

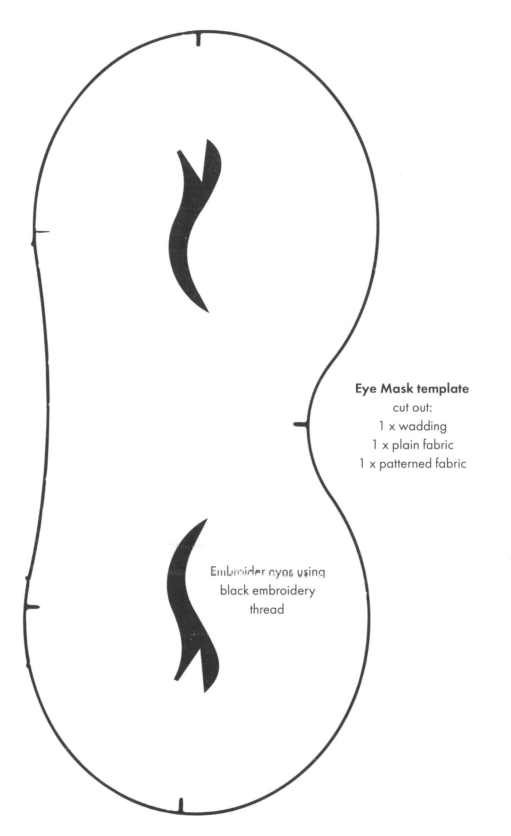

Eye Mask template
cut out:
1 x wadding
1 x plain fabric
1 x patterned fabric

Embroider eyes using
black embroidery
thread

Eye mask template Page 140

About the author

Becci Mai Ford is a craft kit designer, maker and founder of Ellbie Co. She is inspired by all things colourful, happy and kawaii. She lives in Sussex with her husband Mike and their four guinea pigs Crumpet, Nugget, Waffle and Bean who occasionally feature on the Ellbie Co. Instagram account. After living in South Korea for a year in 2014, Becci went on to study advertising at the School of Communication and Art 2.0 in Brixton. It was there that she fell in love with the idea of creating for a living and Ellbie Co. was born. Becci now combines her passion for the cute design style she discovered in South Korea with her love of crafting to create cute and happy mindful craft kits. Becci has sold thousands of craft kits around the world for both individual customers and corporate clients, and she also runs regular crafting workshops teaching cross stitch and embroidery. In 2018 her Kickstarter campaign achieved it's funding goal in under 48 hours and Becci was featured on BBC News, BBC Five Live, BBC Sussex, Cross Stitch Crazy, The World of Cross Stitching and Women Who Create UK.

When she's not working (or stitching) you'll find Becci hula hooping or out running on the Brighton sea front, reading, playing boardgames, baking, chatting for hours with friends and looking for her next piece of colourful inspiration.

Acknowledgements
I would like to thank my husband for his support during the process of writing this book and for photographing each step. I would also like to thank Katherine Raderecht, without whom there would be no book. I'd like to thank my friends, family and the online 'make happy club' community who have supported me and my tiny business from the very beginning.